THE ~~POWER OF GEMS~~
AND CHARMS

BY
GEO. H. BRATLEY

NEWCASTLE PUBLISHING CO, INC
North Hollywood, California
1988

A NEWCASTLE BOOK
First printing, April 1988
10 9 8 7 6 5 4 3 2 1
Printed in the United States of America

PREFACE

VERY one who has the least romance in his soul is interested in charms, though few of the present age have ever troubled themselves to inquire into their origin and history. To openly declare one's belief in such things, whether it be in any ordinary charm, in a gem or jewel, is to lay oneself open to ridicule, if nothing worse. Why is this? The answer must be because of the inability to distinguish between superstition and romance. To rise superior to superstition is progress and enlightenment, but, alas! the day when romance ceases to

exist. Shakespeare, when he wrote,

"The man that hath no music in himself,
Nor is not moved with concord of sweet sounds,
Is fit for treason, stratagems, and spoils,"

might have substituted the word "romance" for "music"; for verily, romance may be said to distinguish the human being from the animal. It is a product of the imagination, and animals have no imagination, so far as we are aware. Every normal human being has this faculty of romance, either latent or active; and if this book can in some measure fructify or strengthen that faculty in its readers, then the writer will consider it has done good work. Let romance grow along with knowledge and the result will be spirituality, but if with ignorance we get superstition.

Here the question will naturally arise : Is the belief in the power of charms all imagination ? To this the writer would emphatically say, No ; and it has been his endeavour to show in the following pages the reason and logic of the power claimed for these things.

But even if this work were but the means of exciting the imagination of its readers into activity, then theirs will be the benefit. Has the reader ever considered what imagination is ? It must not be confused with fancy, for it is the creative or formative power of the mind —a power of the higher soul of man. Imagination with faith and will form the three angles of the triangle of power, without which no creative work or materialisation of thought would be possible ; thus we see that a strong and well organised imagination adds to the creative power of the human mind.

A few years ago wireless telegraphy, aerial navigation, human radiations, and many other achievements of modern science would have been laughed at as the vain imaginings of a superstitious dreamer. To-day these things are labelled science ; therefore the writer ventures to suggest that the efficacy of charms and precious stones may be recognised and placed on a scientific basis before many years are past.

PREFACE

In writing this work, it has been
necessary to borrow from various authors,
ancient and modern, and to these the
writer acknowledges his indebtedness.
Much of the matter in Sections II. and
III. is original, and the outcome of years
of study and investigation.

GEO. H. BRATLEY.

Harrogate.
1906.

CONTENTS

SECTION I

HISTORICAL CHARMS

Chap.   Page

I. JEWELLERY 3

II. GEMS AND COINS 18

III. VASES, GOBLETS, AND WEAPONS   .   . 26

IV. STONES 30

V. BUILDINGS, TREES, AND HERBS .   .   . 36

VI. HUMAN SKULLS 41

VII. HUMAN BEINGS AND ANIMALS .   .   . 46

VIII. DIVERS CHARMS 52

IX. CHARMS IN RELIGION 59

vii

CONTENTS

Chap.   Page

X. CHARMED WELLS AND HOLY WATER . 69

XI. THE HORSESHOE AND SOME OLD-DAY CHARMS 74

XII. SOME CURATIVE CHARMS . . . 80

XIII. SPELLS, OR WRITTEN CHARMS . . 84

XIV. THE INDIVIDUAL, FAMILY, TRIBAL, AND NATIONAL CHARM 91

SECTION II

OCCULT JEWELLERY AND GEMS

When, Where, and How to Use These

XV. WHAT THE WORLD SAYS 97

XVI. DESCRIPTION OF STONES USED AS CHARMS 102

XVII. NATIONS AND THEIR FAVOURITE GEMS 112

XVIII. THE LANGUAGE OF PRECIOUS STONES . 118

XIX. THE PLANETS AND BIRTH-MONTH STONES 127

XX. TALISMANIC ENGRAVED JEWELS . . 132

XXI. LUCKY MASCOTS AND TRINKETS . . 141

XXII. HOW TO WEAR CHARMS AND TALISMANS 144

CONTENTS

SECTION III

THEIR EFFICACY

Ancient and Modern Theories

Chap.		Page
XXIII.	MAGIC	149
XXIV.	ANCIENT OCCULT THEORIES . .	155
XXV.	MODERN SCIENCE AND OCCULT THEORIES	162
XXVI.	NATURE SPIRITS: THE POWER BEHIND THE GEM	166
XXVII.	CLASSIFICATION OF CHARMS . .	170
XXVIII.	GEMS: WHENCE THEIR EFFICACY .	180

SECTION I
HISTORICAL CHARMS

"Then speaks the lord, and waves it light,
  'This glass of flashing crystal tall,
Gave to my sires the Fountain-Sprite;
She wrote in it: *If this glass doth fall,
Farewell then, O Luck of Edenhall!*'"
    —*Longfellow, "The Luck of Edenhall."*

"They have their chrystals, I do know, and rings,
And virgin parchment, and their dead men's skulls,
Their raven wings, their lights, and pentacles,
With characters; I ha' seen all these."
    —*Ben Jonson, "Devil's an Ass," I. 2.*

"All things in earth and air,
  Bound were by magic spell,
Never to do him harm;
Even the plants and stones,
All save the mistletoe—
The sacred mistletoe."
    —*Longfellow, "Tegner's Drapa."*

"And still o'er many a neighbouring door
She saw the horseshoe's curved charm,
To guard against her mother's harm."
    —*Whittier, "The Witch's Daughter."*

2

CHAPTER I

JEWELLERY

AGIC, and not mere æstheticism, was the original motive for wearing jewellery, said Professor Ridgeway to the Anthropological Society in April, 1904. Numerous examples were given which could not leave a doubt that jewellery was always, and is even now, subconsciously worn for its magic properties. Any jewel or gem so worn must be classed as a charm, which word means anything worn to avert ill or secure good fortune. Some prefer the name "mascot," which is the French for a little sorcerer or magician—anything

Motive for wearing jewellery

3

bringing good luck. By this it is clear that the French recognise magic as the power acting through the charm. It is not necessary that the object to which this power is ascribed need be a piece of jewellery ; for charms have taken as many forms in design and material as there have been varieties of magic practised by their use. Minerals, metals, precious stones —indeed, all of Nature's products —may be said to possess this magical property ; while any object may be converted into a charm by one who possessed the necessary knowledge and essential qualifications. Among historical charms we find gems, jewels, coins, vases, goblets, stones, weapons, herbs, trees, skulls, bones, buildings, animals, water, human beings ; there is also that large section called spells, where the charm consists of a formula of words or written characters, often the object and formula being used in conjunction. They may also be classed as individual, family, tribal, and national.

There are numerous stories connected

with our subject, many of these well authenticated, which go to prove that there is more in this branch of magic than is generally supposed. No doubt the truth as to their efficacy is often overlaid with much fiction and nonsense; yet underneath, if we will but search, we may find a stratum of truth which will repay the trouble taken.

We will now see what history has to contribute to our subject.

Rings appear to have been much in evidence in connection with magic, and many are those to which this mysterious faculty is attributed. Solomon is credited with having possessed a ring in which was imprisoned spirits, Rings much who at their master's com- in evidence mand performed the most as charms marvellous acts. Many old legends relate to similar powers being possessed by owners of rings, served by evil spirits, made slaves to man's will by unlawful searching into the forbidden. Apollonius of Tyana is said to have changed his rings daily, using a particular ring with the correct jewel for every day in the week. Speaking of his magical power, Justin Martyr asks, " How is it that the talismans of Apollonius have power in certain members of creation ? ''

There was long preserved in Westminster Abbey a ring which was reported to have been brought to King Edward by persons from Jerusalem : this ring was said to prevent the falling sickness. Cardinal Wolsey was openly accused before the court of confederacy with a man named Wood, a sorcerer, who said that, " My Lord Cardinale had suche a rynge that whatsomever he askyd of the Kynges grace that he hadd yt.'' This case is to be found in the record office of the Rolls House.

The Emperor William of Germany possesses a ring which has a very curious history. It is the talisman of the family. Legend relates that since the **The Emperor William's ring** time of the Elector John of Brandenburgh, every ruler of the House of Hohenzollern has, when dying, if possible, handed a sealed packet to his successor.

This packet contains a ring in which is set a black stone that was dropped by an enormous toad upon the bed of the wife of the Elector immediately after she had given birth to a son, the toad afterwards mysteriously disappearing. The stone was zealously taken care of, and the father of Frederick the Great had it set in a ring. Schneider, the librarian of William I., declares that he witnessed the handing over of the precious packet by Geiling, the treasurer, to his royal master on his accession ; and he further asserts that he read the full account of the stone to the Emperor, who fully confirmed it. The ring has ever since been worn by the head of the House of Hohenzollern. William II. wears it on all great occasions, and he has great respect, like every Hohenzollern, for the curious old jewel. In the archives at Berlin are many documents of that time referring to it.

A well-known story is that of the Spanish opal ; and many are the Spaniards who believe that the long series of

misfortunes that has befallen Spain
and the present dynasty comes of a
cursed opal ring that a neglected
The beauty spitefully bestowed upon
Spanish
opal Alfonso XII. The opal is of a
very large size and of brilliant
colouring. It is set in filigree gold, and
has no other jewels about it. The ring
belonged to a famous beauty and ad-
venturess, the Comtesse de Castiglione,
who was in the glory of her beauty and
power during the reign of Napoleon III.
Among her most ardent admirers was
Alfonso XII., then an outcast and a
pretender. When he became King and
married one of his own royal blood, the
jealousy of the Comtesse was aroused,
and her hatred was terrible. A few
months after the King's marriage he
received a package from the Comtesse,
containing a beautiful opal ring of rare
colouring. It was called a wedding-gift
and a memento of the friendship the
King had held for the Comtesse. The
King showed it to his wife Queen Mer-
cedes, who was charmed with its beauty

and begged to keep it. Alfonso gave it to her readily, and she slipped it on her finger. From that moment she commenced to ail, and in a few months she died. The ring fell from her dead hand, and the King gave it to his grandmother Queen Christina, who died a few months later. Next, the ring was given to Alfonso's sister the Infanta Maria del Pilar, who wore it but a few days before she died of a mysterious sickness. The sister-in-law then came into possession of it, the youngest daughter of the Duc and Duchesse de Montpensier, and in three months the young Princess was dead. After this series of fatalities the King determined to keep the ring himself, and he slipped it on his little finger ; but he did not wear it long, as his unhappy life shortly came to an end. Queen Christina, who is not in any way superstitious, took possession of the ring after her husband's death, but the other members of the family begged her to destroy it ; this she refused to do, but attached the fatal ring to a gold chain, which she hung round the neck of the Virgin of Almudena, the patron saint of Madrid.

Not content with the evil influence of the cursed opal, Spain possesses another piece of jewellery of deadly maleficence. "Mephisto's ring," as it is called, is a gold ring set with a large emerald, the centre of which has been hollowed out and contains a ruby, surrounded with tiny diamonds. It came to Spain (no one knows from whence) in the reign of Philip II., and following its arrival, came the succession of calamities which brought about the decline of Spanish power. To those who owned the ring it seemed to bring personal disaster ; and at the time of the Spanish American war it was presented by the Spanish royal family to a church, possibly in the hope that its baneful influence would be thus neutralised. The church was burned to the ground, but the ring was saved, and this time given to a museum. The museum was afterwards struck by lightning twice, and the return

"Mephisto's ring," brings ill-luck to Spain

of the ring to the royal family was followed by the defeat of the Spanish army and navy. The ring has now been placed in a strong box and buried.

The Czar of Russia is said to be very superstitious and to have great confidence in relics. He wears a ring in which is embedded a piece of the true cross, and it is said to have the virtue of shielding its wearer from any physical danger. It was originally one of the treasures of the Vatican, and was presented to an ancestor of the Czar for diplomatic reasons. The value which its owner sets upon the ring is shown by the fact that he will never, if possible, move any distance without it. Some years ago he was travelling from St. Petersburg to Moscow when he suddenly discovered he had forgotten the ring. The train was stopped immediately, and a special messenger sent back in an express for it ; nor would the Czar allow the train to move until eight hours afterwards, when the messenger returned with the ring. It is said that when his ill-fated grandfather was so cruelly assassinated he had left the ring behind him.

The Czar has also another ring with a more pleasant history to it, the story is both pretty and romantic. It is a plain ring and of a quaint Gothic design. The ring was given to Princess Charlotte of Prussia, daughter of Frederick William III., by her governess, while the Princess was still a schoolgirl. On the inside of it in faint characters, the words " Russia's Czarina " are just legible. Many years later Prince Nicholas of Russia, then without any hope of succeeding to the throne, saw and fell in love with the young Princess, and, during dinner, on the first evening of their meeting, begged her to give him a little remembrance as a sign that his love was returned. " Pray give me that little ring," he whispered ; and secretly it was handed to him. Eight years later the prophetic words engraved within the ring came true. Nicholas became Czar of Russia and Charlotte its Czarina.

Napoleon I. had great faith in a ring
which he always wore. At the time of
his abdication at Fontainebleau in 1814,
and after his unsuccessful attempt
to poison himself, he said to Dr. The fated
Corvisart, who attended him, ring of
" I was not meant to die ; I Napoleon I.
did not think of my talisman."
So saying, he pointed to his ring which
he is supposed to have received from a
priest after the Nile Expedition. After
his death the ring was transferred to
Queen Hortense.

The same ring played a part in the life
of young Prince Imperial, who met his
death in Zululand in 1879. His father
Napoleon III. became the possessor of
the ring previously mentioned and wore
it constantly. When he died it was
proposed that the ring should be removed
and worn by his son. When the Prince
refused to have this done, it was freely
prophesied that evil would come of it,
and subsequent events go to show that
these predictions were realised.

But it is not only royalty who believe

in the magic of charms, for we find the great composer Hadyn had a ring which was his source of inspiration. Without the ring he could rack his brain in vain for melodies : with it the music would leap to his fingers.

Hadyn's inspiration due to a charmed ring

Mr. Rider Haggard, the novelist, wears a quaint signet ring which once adorned the finger of that Pharaoh who made Israel captive, and to this ornament the novelist ascribes many virtues.

M. Santos Dumont, the conqueror of the air, is stated to attribute his providential escape from injury in 1901 to the fact that he was wearing on his wrist a bracelet to which hangs a medal of St. Benoit, given him by the Countess D'Eu.

M. Santos Dumont's bracelet

Miss Yvonne Lamor, the young Spanish protégée of the late King of Servia, wears a curious tortoiseshell brooch which has an interesting history. It was, it seems, given to the King Milan by his mother. He in turn gave it to King Alexander.

A few days before his assassination, the King sent for Miss Lamor and gave her the brooch. "Wear it as a mascot," he said. "When you have it on you will have good luck." She has worn it daily ever since.

The well-known jeweller, Mr. Streeter, of Bond Street, though not afraid to walk under ladders, spill salt, and do other unlucky things, always carries attached to his watch-chain a small, quaint, sharply carved seal which was originally found in an Egyptian coffin. He has worn it for many years, and says he would not be without it for anything.

The clever black-and-white artist Mr. Austin Osman Spare once picked up a golden skull, bearing the word "One " in opals.

A blackand-white artist's golden skull

On the night he picked it up he dreamed that as long as he kept the trinket he would be lucky. So far his dream has come true. It is for this reason that he signs his drawings "One."

Miss Kellermann, the swimmer, possesses a little mascot in the shape of the model of a diver.

Madame Esty never appears in public without a small green heart, which is attached to a delicate necklace of gold. She also values highly an antique topaz trophy, which she has converted into a brooch. This stone was once possessed by a famous Indian necromancer. By appealing to its power he was able to command the appearance of food and drink. One night he lay by the side of a suffering comrade on the battlefield. He himself was wounded by a dart. He heard his comrade moaning in an agony of thirst, and, taking the charm from his bosom, threw it to the side of the sufferer, saying, " Wear it near thy heart if thy parched throat would find relief,'' and fell back dead. The strange command was obeyed, and when at dawn the grateful soldier looked for his benefactor, no trace could be found. With this legend it was thought to be especially appropriate in the possession of a singer, and Madame Esty regards it with due reverence.

Mrs. Nicholas Longworth's favourite ornament is a beautiful jade necklace. which was given to her when she visited the Empress of China. The Empress herself decorated Miss Roosevelt with the necklace, and told her that the linked bits of stone were very old, that they had been cut by an artist who had the reputation of being one half wizard, and that the ornament would bring to its owner her heart's desire. Of the many rich and curious gifts which Miss Roosevelt received during her tour, this was the only one which she kept for herself and wore constantly. After her engagement to Congressman Nicholas Longworth was made public, she confided to some of her friends that she believed there really was virtue in the necklace.

CHAPTER II

GEMS AND COINS

EMS are so beautiful and possess such a mysterious fascination for the human mind, that it is in no way surprising that they should have received so large a share of attention from the earliest periods of human history.

A large sapphire figures as the mascot of the Jews ; the same stone is believed to have been the signet of the wise Solomon.

It is supposed that this stone has its home in the Holy of Holies, the very centre of the ark. It is much mixed up with the fortunes of the Jews, and was nearly lost to them at the sacking of Jerusalem by the Roman Titus. Around it is built

The mascot of the Jews

the story of the Wandering Jew, Cartaphilus ; while we find it mentioned in a story of Cornelius Agrippa, the famed magician.

One of the most famous diamonds is the " Koh-i-Noor,'' which is said to have been found near the Krishna river, and to have been worn more than five thousand years ago by Karhma, one of the heroes celebrated in the Mahabharatha. In the course of centuries it often changed hands. In 1560 it was in the possession of Baber, the founder of the Mogul dynasty. In 1665 it is reputed to have weighed 280 carats, but as it has so often been recut, it is impossible to say what its original weight was. It was of such immense value as a charm that one rajah who owned it is A fortune stated to have refused £100,000 refused for offered by the Governor of India. the "Koh-i-Noor" The rajah said that the fortunes of his family were bound up with the stone, and he would not risk them by parting with it. One virtue ascribed to this diamond is that the water in which

it was placed would cure all diseases.
When the Punjaub came under British
rule the stone was presented to Queen
Victoria, who had it recut for the last
time. It is now the property of Queen
Alexandra.

Another celebrated diamond is one
which was in the possession of the late
President **President Kruger, and his mis-**
Kruger's fortunes were believed by many
unlucky to be due to this stone. At one
diamond time it belonged to Chaka, a Zulu
chief. Chaka himself owned it till
his assassination by his brother, who then
entered into possession. The brother was
himself assassinated, and within a few
years the diamond changed hands fifteen
times, and in every case the owner died
a violent death.

There are four rubies in existence which
have brought misfortune on generations
of their possessor. One almost destroyed
a native state in India, so that the people
with all due ceremony removed it to
the Himalayas and buried it secretly.
Another has brought disaster on a

Russian house. It had been brought to England, but returned to assist in the St. Petersburg riots and massacres. Cubans are now searching for a third which has involved that distressful island in calamities, and the fourth is in Egypt, where it surely merits the attention of Lord Cromer.

The name of those who place faith in coins from the value of a farthing to a guinea is legion. Any one who has come into contact with gamesters or sporting-men will know how many of this class keep their lucky coin to win the lucky toss, or how such a coin is reverently preserved, so that it may bring luck in any hazardous undertaking. At Berwick, a fisherman was charged with stealing the " lucky " coin from a fishing vessel. It was stated that a shilling was given to the vessel some years ago by a local gentleman, and the coin had been nailed to a beam in the cabin for good luck. But not only as bringers of luck are coins noted, for perhaps the most famous coin is

Coins as charms; the Penny of Lee

that known as "The Penny of Lee," which has been rendered famous by Sir Walter Scott's work, "The Talisman." The story of this coin is that Sir Simon Lockhart, a friend of and knighted by Robert Bruce, went on a crusade, and while in the Holy Land took a Saracen chief prisoner. The wife of the latter came to ransom her husband, and while paying over the money, dropped a small silver coin with a precious stone in the centre ; this the canny Scot at once picked up and kept. This is the famed "Penny," and a remarkable point about it is that it has the property of curing any ailment of man or beast. It is only necessary to immerse the coin in water and for the patient to drink this. How highly it was valued for this purpose is shown by the fact that, during the plague of 1665, the town of Carlisle borrowed the charm, depositing securities valued at thousands of pounds for its safe return !

The Russian Czar has recently come into possession of some charmed coins. Bernhard Tutnauer, a Jew, who lives at

Radautz, a town in the Austrian crown-land Bakevina, had, as a guest, three years ago, a wonder-working rabbi from the Orient. On de- Charmed parting, the rabbi rewarded the coins sent to the Czar hospitality shown him with by a Jew some coins, saying, "My son, although these pieces may seem a poor gift, they will protect those far greater than you in time of danger." For three nights in succession the vision of Alexander III., the Czar's father, appeared to Tutnauer, and told him the rabbi's coins would shield any one who wears a crown from violent death. Tutnauer sent the coins to the Russian Charge d'Affaires at Vienna, with a message which vividly described his triple dream. The Charge appeared visibly impressed, and undertook to have the magical coins sent to the Czar, who, on receiving them, sent a message to Tutnauer, thanking him for the mascot.

Some time previous to King Alfonso's visit to England he encountered an old gipsy woman, to whom he offered some douros, but which were haughtily refused. "King," said the woman, "keep thy money. My race is older than thine. I am the last of the Almoravides, who ruled over Morocco and the south of Spain in the eleventh and twelfth centuries. It is I, on the contrary, who will present thee with a piece of gold." With this the gipsy offered the King a sequin, bearing the effigy of Ishag, son of Tachefin, the last of the kings of the Almoravides. "Take good care of this talisman," she added; "it will guard thee against all dangers. There exists only one other sequin like it. I gave it to an exquisitely beautiful and highly charitable young lady when I fell into a ditch one day. I was badly wounded, and she dismounted and bound up my forehead with her handkerchief. Those who accompanied her addressed her as her highness. King, if ever thou shouldst marry, wed only this young girl, she alone can make thee happy." This story is spoken about a good deal in Madrid, and

King Alfonso and the gipsy woman's talisman

it is asserted that the King was just showing the sequin to M. Loubet when the bomb was thrown at him on his last official visit to Paris. The talisman thus saved his life. The story also goes that when in London the King

Princess Ena possesses the second sequin

ascertained that the other golden sequin was in possession of Princess Ena of Battenberg, whom he has since taken as his Queen.

CHAPTER III

VASES, GOBLETS, AND WEAPONS

ORE than one family's luck is connected with a vase or goblet. Edenhall, Penrith, Cumberland, is the home of Sir Richard and the Hon. Lady Musgrave, whose mascot is in the form of a cup or vase of crystal,

The charmed cup of Edenhall

said to be one of the oldest glasses in England. Legend tells how the butler, having gone to bring water from the well, called St. Cuthbert's, near the hall, surprised a party of fairies dancing on the lawn. They had left their cup lying upon the grass. The butler seized hold of it, and though called upon to restore it, he ran toward the hall, hearing this couplet as he ran :

" If e'er that cup should break or fall,
Farewell the luck of Edenhall."

This cup is guarded with the most jealous care, and has attained world-wide celebrity, partly because of its antiquity, though probably more through Longfellow's poem.

Another family, that of Muncaster, possesses a goblet, claimed to be the one which King Henry VI. drank from when he was sheltered from his pursuers by Sir John Pennington in the year 1461. The welfare of the family is believed to depend on the safety of this goblet. During the great Civil War a careless servant dropped the box in which it was kept, and we are told that for more than fifty years afterwards no one of the family dared to open the case to see whether the goblet was injured or not. At last a young heir was bold enough to risk it. The case was unlocked, and, to the delight of all concerned, it was

The Muncaster mascot

discovered that the Muncaster mascot had not received the slightest damage.

Many are the weapons said to be invested with magical qualities. There is a strange dread existing amongst reigning houses that the existence of the innocent but unhallowed weapons by which rulers have been assassinated is fraught with peril to their descendants. Most of these weapons are now destroyed.

Superstition regarding weapons

The Shah of Persia has a diamond set in a scimitar, which renders its possessor invincible. He has also a dagger with the same property, but it is ordained that those who use it shall perish by it, so it is carefully kept shut up in a sandal-wood box on which is engraved a verse from the Koran.

Mr. C. W. Leadbeater in his work, " The Other Side of Death,'' tells a story of a charmed dagger. He says : " A friend of mine has a dagger which was said to have the gruesome property of inspiring any one who took hold of it with a longing to kill some woman. My friend was sceptical, but still eyed the dagger a little doubtfully; for when he had himself taken hold of it, he felt so queer that he had to quickly put it down again. There seemed no doubt that at least two women had, as a matter of fact, been murdered with it.'' Mr. Leadbeater, who is a clairvoyant of the first grade, took the dagger away to experiment with, and experienced a curious kind of dragging sensation. He looked to see what it was, and saw a wild-looking man who seemed very angry at his not going where he was trying to push him. This man, through a faithless wife, had sworn revenge against the whole sex, and had killed his wife, his wife's sister, and another woman before he himself was killed. He had attached himself to the dagger, and had met with some success in tempting its various owners to murder women. The dagger was broken up and buried.

An obsessed dagger

A charmed dagger kills three women

CHAPTER IV

STONES

CERTAIN stones are said to be fated for luck or otherwise, and we find these ranging from those worn as ornaments to those weighing many tons. Among the former class is one belonging to the famous Lady Ellenborough, known among the Arabs of Damascus and in the desert, after her last marriage, as Hanoum Medjouye. It was presented to her by a Druze from Mount Lebanon. This charm is a green stone of a pentagonal form : at the bottom is engraved a fish ; higher, Solomon's seal ; and still higher, the four Chaldaic letters which form the name of the Deity.

There are many strange stories connected with this stone.

It is commonly thought that Mr. Leopold de Rothschild owes his luck in winning the Derby with St. Amant to a little green stone, carved in the shape of a Hindoo god, which he carries about with him ; though it is suspected that his luck was strengthened on the above occasion through a soap-stone which some one anonymously sent him with a letter saying that it often brought its owners luck. The little Hindoo god and the Derby

Mr. B. L. Farjeon, the novelist, wears a little green stone on his watch-chain, which he picked up many years ago in New Zealand, and which is supposed to hold the eminent writer's luck.

Madame H. P. Blavatsky had in her possession a carnelian stone of a magical nature. Writing of the Shamans of Tartary, she says, that they all have such a stone, which they wear attached to a string and carry under the left arm. On one occasion she was witness to some weird sights and doings, brought about by a Shaman through one of these charmed stones, who appeared to be able to separate his astral body from the physical, and travel in this at the bidding of her unspoken wish.

Among those stones which places them outside of the category of jewellery or ornaments, we must name the **The stone** Coronation Stone in Westminster **mascot of** Abbey. Enclosed in the seat **England** of St. Edward's chair, it is a stone to which some peculiar properties are attributed. It is asserted to be the same which the Patriarch rested his head upon in the plain of Luza, and is said to have been carried first to Brigantia, a city of Gallicia in Spain. From thence Simon Brech brought it into Ireland : he lived about seven hundred years before Christ, and was the first King of the Scots. From there, about three hundred and seventy years later, it was taken into Scotland by King Fergus. In the year 850 A.D. King Kenneth placed it in the Abbey of Scone, this being the place where the Scottish kings were usually crowned. In the year 1297 it was brought into England by King Edward I., and placed in Westminster Abbey. The tradition is that it murmurs approval at the coronation when the rightful heir assumes his or her seat on it. It was, in former times, carried at the head of the army as a mascot of victory, and the hooks by which it was suspended still remain.

Some curious stories attach to the stones on Stonehenge, one of these is that when one of the large stones fall a sovereign will die ; and it is said that only a few days before the death of Queen Victoria one of the *Stonehenge and the* great blocks which help to form *death of* the old Druid temple fell from *Queen Victoria* its place during a severe gale.

In the island of Fladda Chuan there is a chapel, dedicated to St. Columbus. On an altar a round blue stone rests, which is always moist. The fishermen wash this stone to procure a favourable wind. There is another stone in Iona over which if a man stretches his arm three times he will never err in steering a vessel.

In the island of Bernora there is a stone in the form of a cross. At one time it was the custom of the natives to erect it when they wished rain, and to lay it flat on the ground for dry weather. From this it derived the name of the water cross. A green stone about the size of a goose egg was the pride of the island of Arran. By laying it on the side of a person troubled with pain in that part of the body, the patient immediately recovered, unless the patient was doomed to die, when the stone would move of its own accord from the side.

Just beside the chief gate of the Imperial Palace of Mukden stands an insignificant black stone. It is nothing to look at, and one might pass it a dozen times without attaching any importance to it. It is an ordinary shaft of black basalt, eighteen inches high, octagonal in shape, old and worn. This stone is to

The black stone of the Chinese

the Manchurian race the mascot of their imperial position ; and the legend runs that, when the Chinese dynasty loses possession of the black stone of Mukden, it will lose the throne of China as well.

The celebrated Dr. Dee possessed a charmed stone of which he made inquiries as to the future. This charm came into the keeping of Horace Walpole, and was long, if not now, in the Strawberry Hill collection.

CHAPTER V

BUILDINGS, TREES, AND HERBS

N all parts of the world there are houses that are practically unletable on account of weird legends attaching to them. "Give a dog a bad name and hang him," is an old saw which many owners of property could easily paraphrase and then apply it to certain houses they possess and to which an ill-fate appears to attach ; for when this has once established itself, then the owner might as well raze the house to the ground. Ill luck or its opposite may be said to be built into a house, and it is seldom that those who

erect costly mansions for their own use
live long to occupy them, sometimes it
is death, or it may be ruin, that overtakes
its owner.

" Unlucky Dalham,'' otherwise Dalham
Hall, Suffolk, where the late Colonel Frank
Rhodes died, is only one of the many
examples of houses with reputations for
bringing misfortune upon their possessors.

It is only recently that a well-known
man, for superstitious reasons, it is said,
refused to occupy a beautiful house he
had built until some one else, a perfect
stranger, had lived in it for some little
time. We even find an intellectual man
like the late Lord Salisbury leasing a
splendid house he had built Lord
for himself at Beaulieu on the Salisbury
Riviera to strangers for several and his
months before he or any of house at
his family would consent to Beaulieu
occupy it.

The completion of Lord Revelstoke's
palace in Charles Street coincided with the
bankruptcy of the great firm of Baring
Brothers of which he was the principal,

and the house stands as a monument to the futility of human ambition.

The Empress Eugénie's sister, the late Duchess of Alba, only occupied the palace erected for her in the Champs Elysees a few months before she was seized with a sudden illness, and died in a mysterious manner which gave rise to curious rumours. The palace was subsequently pulled down.

In history we find that there are some trees, herbs, and vegetables to which this mysterious faculty has been ascribed, and which appear to have some strange affinity with individuals and families.

Aubrey, in his writings, says, " I cannot omit taking notice of the great misfortune in the family of the Earl of Winchelsea, who, at Eastwell in Kent, felled down a most curious grove of trees near his own noble seat and gave the first blow with his own hands.   Shortly after his countess died in her bed suddenly, and his eldest son, the Lord Maidstone, was killed at sea by a cannon ball.''

Strange properties possessed by trees

At Bretley, near Burton-on-Trent, the old seat of the Stanhopes, and now of Lord Carnarvon, by inheritance in the female line, the charmed tree is a fine old cedar near the hall from whence a bough falls when a death occurs in the family. It is stated that this tree is now chained up and banded with iron.

For several hundred years it has been affirmed that prior to the death of an Earl of Seafield, there is a violent storm ; and a fir tree, which is the crest of the Grants, is invariably uprooted and cast to the ground with its head lying in the direction of the Seafield's residence.

Many people will have heard of the Coalstoun Pear ; this fruit was given as a talisman on her wedding day to the daughter and heiress of the family by a wizard more than three centuries ago, with the injunction that *Financial disaster through biting a pear* it was never to be eaten or cut. At the close of the eighteenth century the wife of the head of the family, out of curiosity, bit a piece out of the fruit. At once came financial disaster, and part of the property had to be sold. The remains of the pear, now shrunk to the size of a marble, are carefully preserved in a silver casket.

The mandrake, perhaps unsurpassed for its mystic qualities, is said to bring good luck to those who possess it. It is regarded as a species of elf in France, and Joan of Arc is thought to have owed her victories to a mandrake root.

CHAPTER VI

HUMAN SKULLS

HERE are many charmed skulls in existence at the present day, and perhaps one connected with Burton Agnes Hall is the most celebrated. This hall is the country seat of the Boyntons. In the time of Elizabeth the hall and estates became vested in three sisters, co-heiresses, who determined to have erected for themselves and their descendants the present mansion instead of the older building. The younger of the three sisters, who had taken special interest in the erection of the new house, A weird story of Burton Agnes Hall

was brutally maltreated by some ruffians when paying a visit to Harpham Hall, the residence of Lady St. Quentin, and died very shortly after. Before her death, she made her sisters promise that her head should be removed from her body and preserved within the hall, to remain there for ever. She also left a weird message to future owners of the house that if they disobeyed these injunctions she would render the place unhabitable. Her sisters, who had only made the promise to pacify her, had the body interred in the church without decapitation. A very short time afterwards, such disturbances took place that the servants refused to remain in the hall, and it became, in truth, impossible to live there. The two sisters then consulted with the vicar of the parish, and had the coffin brought up from the vault, and, on opening it, found the head severed from the body, and rapidly assuming the appearance of a fleshless skull. The skull was duly brought to the house and placed on a table in the hall, where, with the exception of very short periods, it has remained ever since. On one occasion the Boynton of the day, ignoring or disbelieving his ancestress's power to make things unpleasant, caused the skull to be buried in the garden. The result was that dreadful wailings and numerous crashings were heard about the hall, and the skull had to be taken up again.

At Bettiscombe House, near Bridport, in Dorsetshire, there is a charmed human relic known as the "Screaming Skull"; it is said to be that of a negro, though the true history of the skull does not appear to be known. Tradition The "Screaming says that the negro had de-Skull" of clared before his death that if Bettiscombe House his body was not taken to his native land his spirit would not rest. The body was buried, but such disturbances took place in the house that it had to be taken up for peace and quietness. The skeleton has gradually disappeared, but the skull remains, and is kept as a charm.

Another skull is preserved for similar reasons at Tunstead Farm, near Chapel-on-le-Frith, in Derbyshire. This is a female skull, and if it is removed everything on the farm goes wrong. The inhabitants of the locality have many tales to tell of its mystical performances.

Wardley Hall, near Manchester, is noted for its possession of an unburied human skull. It is supposed to be the skull of Roger Downe, who was the heir to the property ; but having met his death in a brawl in London, his head was sent to his sister, and this head has been kept at the hall ever since, for any one trying to get rid of it is punished severely—indeed, it is stated that, do what they will, it is always sure to return. The place has changed hands many times, but each succeeding tenant endures the skull's presence rather than put up with the annoyances and terrors which take place on its removal.

A skull which intends to stay

At the Old Manor House, Knaresborough, in Yorkshire, there is a haunted room called the Blue Bedroom, the door of which cannot be kept closed. It has been locked and a chair placed against it, but to no purpose, for in the morning it is found open. When the house was restored a few years ago, and the position of the staircase was altered, the skeleton of a woman was unearthed. The skull is kept in the house and would appear to have something to do with the nightly visitant.

CHAPTER VII

HUMAN BEINGS AND ANIMALS

IT is a well-established belief that some human beings possess, it may be unconsciously, this same strange power, and are notably lucky or unlucky to those they come into close contact with.

It is stated that the Rothschilds **Men and women as charms** will never employ a man if they know him to have been unlucky. The writer of this work is acquainted with a man who boasts of his power as a mascot for good luck to any one who has dealings with him.

In society Lady Bancroft was always

credited with the power of being a mascot ; so much was this believed that many of her friends begged some object from her that she had worn, and to these favoured ones she usually gave a shoe.

Examples of human beings who act as unlucky forces are numerous, and probably the most prominent of these are to be found among those of royal blood who have adopted a seafaring life as a profession. Among these may be mentioned the Grand Duke Alexis, the Duke of Coburg his brother-in-law, Archduke John, of Austria, and the Prince of Leiningen.

Royal sailors who give ill-luck

Mr. Darnborough, the successful American player at Monte Carlo, appears to have discovered two human charms. We are told that his luck changed when he substituted a gold pig as a luck-bringer for the two young ladies who always accompanied him as mascots when he played. When he first went to the Casino, he would not play unless he had one of these

Two human mascots at the Monte Carlo gaming-tables

ladies on each side and a number of stacks of gold pieces in front. Suddenly, he changed his tactics. The ladies disappeared, and he put a little gold pig on the table in front of him. Since then he has had little luck.

This same mystic force will often attach itself to a name, irrespective of the temperament of the individual bearing it. In 1664, on December 5th, the ship " Menai " was crossing the Straits, and capsized in a gale. Eighty-one passengers were on board, and only one was saved. His name was Hugh Williams. On December 5th, 1785, a schooner was wrecked on the Isle of Man. Sixty persons were aboard, among them one Hugh Williams and his family. Only one survived the shock, and that was old Hugh Williams. On August 5th, 1820, a picnicing party on the Thames was run down by a coal barge. Of the twenty-five picnicers, most of whom were under twelve years of age, only one child, aged five, returned to tell the tale. His name

The charmed name of Hugh Williams

was Hugh Williams. On August 19th, 1889, a Leeds coal barge, with nine men, foundered. Two of them were rescued by some fishermen. They were an uncle and his nephew, and both were named Hugh Williams.

Turning to animals, we find that the black cat is held in high favour as a luck bringer in Italy ; while many people in England look upon it_{The black} as a good omen when a strange_{cat as a} black cat comes and takes up_{luck-bringer} its residence in the house.

At Cowes, the Kaiser's Cup was won by the *Satanita*, with Sir Maurice Fitzgerald's black cat on board.

Three black cats are stated to have been taken by Dr. Barton, the aeronaut, on one of his trips, these were carried as luck-bringers.

Mdlle. Nathalie Janotha, court pianist to the German Emperor, possesses a mascot in the form of a cat, which is black, but answers to the name of White-Heather. This cat wears a golden necklet, which has been blessed by the Pope, and he possesses gifts innumerable, for he has visited nearly every European Court, and a tuft of his hair is in possession of most of the crowned heads, who keep it as a charm. One day, while Mdlle. Janotha was playing to Mr. Gladstone, during his last illness, this favoured cat entered the room with a sprig of white heather in his mouth, which he presented to the aged statesman.

In the Park of Chartley, near Lichfield, a seat of the Ferrers family, was preserved a species of wild cattle. Their colour was white, muzzles black ; the whole of the inside of the ear and about one-third of the outside, from the tip downwards, red ; horns white, with black tips. It is recorded that in the year when the battle of Burton Bridge was fought and lost, that a black calf was born in this herd, and the downfall of the house of Ferrers happened about the same time. The belief was that the birth of a black or dark-hued calf from this wild herd was a sure sign of death within the same year to a member of the Ferrers family. The

The wild cattle of Chartley

Staffordshire Chronicle of July, 1835, says that a calf of this description has been born whenever a death has happened in the family of late years.

The mascot of the *Renown*, the vessel which conveyed the Prince and Princess of Wales to India in 1905, was a rabbit, which died on the voyage and was consigned to the waves of the Bay of Biscay.

CHAPTER VIII

DIVERS CHARMS

THOSE readers who have visited the British Museum may have noticed a mummy case, No. 22,542. This case has a strange story attached to it. All those whose hands it has passed through have in some manner or other come under the curse of the Priestess of Amen-Ra, whose body, or mummy, the case has been the covering to. Though the mummy still rests in its native land one of the hands was brought to England. Among the list of the remarkable occurrences which befell those who were connected

The spell of the Egyptian mummy case, now in the British Museum

with it were four serious accidents and four conflagrations.

Hintlesham Hall, Colonel Lloyd Anstruther's place in Suffolk, is a very quaint old house, and has the reputation of being haunted. A long time ago the second wife of a former owner was very jealous of her little stepson, and starved him to death. After his death a model in wax was made from his features, which is now kept locked up in one of the rooms. It is called the "Luck of Hintlesham"; for tradition says that if it is broken or harmed in any way, Hintlesham will pass from the family.

Perhaps one of the most gruesome charms on record was worn by Jean Caviglioli, the famous Corsican bandit, who was captured near Ajaccio. In the early days of his career, An assassin Caviglioli slew a rival bandit makes a with his poniard, and, cutting off watch-chain of his his beard, made a watch-chain victim's of it. This he wore for several beard years, and he ascribed to it all the luck he experienced. It is reported that the day on which he was captured was the only one on which he had failed to wear this charm.

The Marquis of Ripon, who, though a Roman Catholic, yet traces his descent back to Oliver Cromwell, possesses a curious relic of his ancestor. When the body of the Lord Protector was taken from its resting-place in Westminster Abbey, in order to be decapitated and buried under the gallows of Tyburn, there was attached to it an inscription on a metal plate. This plate passed to the daughter of the sergeant, who was entrusted with the horrible task, and came into the hands of the Ripon family, where it has remained since as a mascot.

A stream which is connected with the fortunes of the family is to be found on the estates of the Countess of Cromartie. Some time ago she lost her little child, and what made the death more than usually tragic is, that it seemed to be the fulfilment of an old prophecy, which was to the effect that when this stream was turned the estates would in future not go in direct succession ; and it happened that

A fated stream of water

some alterations or improvements had been made on her property which entailed this being done.

The Black Bed of the Otway family, which the owners will not part with for any price, is another mysterious possession. It is a gigantic four-poster made of ebony and beautifully carved. A peculiarity of it is that all its furniture is as black as night.

A curious story is told of the late President Kruger. Many years ago the President bought from an old half-breed woman pedlar a meerschaum pipe, to which she ascribed the power of foretelling the future. The old woman predicted that three important changes in his life would be foretold by accidents befalling the pipe. *The charmed pipe of President Kruger* Early in the year 1881, before the independence of the Transvaal was modified, the stem came to pieces ; a little before the Jameson Raid he chipped a piece of the bowl ; just before his departure for the Bloemfontein Conference the pipe fell to the ground, and was smashed to fragments.

In Laing's "Travels among Timanni, the Kourankos, and the Soulimas," there is a description by an English traveller of a very curious scene. A body of picked soldiers fired upon a chief who had nothing to defend himself with **Bullet-proof men** but certain charms. Although their muskets were properly loaded and aimed not a ball could strike him.

A similar case is given by Salverte, in his "Philosophy of Occult Sciences," where, in 1568, the Prince of Orange condemned a Spanish prisoner to be shot at Juliers. The soldiers tied him to a tree and fired, but he was not hurt. They at last stripped him to see what armour he wore, but found only an amulet. When this was taken from him he fell dead at the first shot.

Nelson, the hero of Trafalgar, had great faith in the luck of a **Nelson's horseshoe** horseshoe, and one was nailed to the mast of the ship *Victory*.

Among the numerous charms possessed by the Shah of Persia may be mentioned

a gold star called Merzoum, which has
the reputation of making conspirators
immediately confess. Another important
one is a cube of amber ; this is supposed
to render the Shah invulnerable, and he
wears it about his neck. A third charm
is a little box of gold, set in emeralds, and
blessed by the prophet.

We must not pass the famous Rothschild talisman, which is an heirloom,
and on the possession of which
the fortunes of the family are   The talis-
thought to depend. It is in the   man of the Rothschild
form of a small gold casket,   family
about the size of a snuff-box,
but the secret of its power lies hidden in
words inscribed within.

Lord Bacon was of opinion that if a
man wore a planet seal it might aid
him in obtaining the affections of his
sweetheart, give him protection at sea
and in battle, and make him more
courageous.

When at Paris, Lord Verulam had his
hands covered with warts. They were
removed by the English ambassador's

wife, who resorted to a charm for this purpose.

The famous wrestler, known as the "Terrible Turk," has a charm which was placed round his neck by his father ; this charm never leaves him, for whether wrestling or sleeping he always wears it.

The "Terrible Turk" wears a charm

At a meeting of the Cheshire Football Association, it was reported that a Barnton player, when taking part in a league match at Davenham, had the misfortune to break his leg, and that another player attached to the same club had also fractured a limb a fortnight later. As both men had worn the same pair of boots, the club's officials believed that there was an affinity between the second and the first accident, and promptly ordered the destruction of the boots.

The Macleods of Dunvegan Castle, Syke, possess a fairy flag, said to be powerful when waved to avert any misfortune to the family.

CHAPTER IX

CHARMS IN RELIGION

F we turn to the various religions of the world, we find that a belief in a magical power, such as has been ascribed to amulets, charms, etc., has prevailed in some form or another, and even does at the present day. Either it is the belief in the miraculous power of relics, idols, consecrated water, or some of the other numerous so-called superstitions found among the many religions and the different races. In a work of this kind it is only possible to give a few historical references from a vast number of cases which could, if space permitted, be gathered together.

Descendants of Abraham believed that

their great ancestor wore, suspended from his neck, a precious stone, the sight of which cured every disease.

Josephus maintains that the precious stones of Aaron's breast-plate were the Urim and Thummin, and that these possessed certain properties so that they discovered or pre-dicted the issue of events to those who consulted them.

The precious stones on Aaron's breast-plate foretell the future

Many people are of opinion that the earrings which Jacob buried under the oak of Sechem were charms; while we have already seen that Solomon was the possessor of a magic ring.

Again, in the Western scriptures, Acts xix. 11, 12, we read : " And God wrought special miracles by the hands of Paul : so that from his body were brought unto the sick handkerchiefs or aprons, and the diseases departed from them, and the evil spirits went out of them.''

Charmed handker-chiefs in the Western scriptures

It is quite probable that St. John alludes to the white carnelian, a gem well known among adepts for its occult properties, when he says, " To him that overcometh will I give to eat of the hidden manna, and will give him a white stone, and in the stone a new name written, which no man knoweth saving he that receiveth it '' (Rev. ii. 17).

Religiously disposed Jews wore charms written on parchment upon their arms or foreheads. The sacred word Jehovah read in a certain way was said to produce miraculous effects.

In the Roman Catholic Church there is much material which we may draw upon. At one time, if it was necessary to extinguish a fire or stop an inundation, the holy father threw a consecrated wafer into the midst of the flames or overflowing river, while conse-crated oil was regarded as an infallible charm and love-philter.

Love-philters, and vests proof against violence

A holy vest was a gift often made by the Pope to protect the wearer from violence of every description. These vests gave the wearers courage in the hour of danger, and no weapon had power to harm them.

It was the custom at one time for the Popes to send a golden key to faithful priests, wherein was enclosed a small quantity of the filings of St. Peter's keys, kept sacred at Rome. These charms were worn in the bosom to protect the happy possessor from disease, misfortune, and evil spirits.

It is stated that an angel delivered a written charm to one of the Popes, and directed him to take it to King Charles when he went to the battle of Roncesvalles. The holy messenger said that whoever carried a copy of this writing, and every day said three paternosters, three aves, and one creed, would be saved from all enemies and dangers.

A written charm given to King Charles at the battle of Roncesvalles

The charmed tomb of Abbé Paris, a Jansenist, who died in 1727, is worthy of mention. Hume, in his Philosophical Essays, says, " There surely never was so great a number of miracles ascribed to one person as those which were lately said to have been wrought in France upon the tomb of the Abbé Paris.''

To-day we have a charm of great value

in the Holy Coat of Treves, which is perhaps the most famous of all the various religious charms; its magical properties being attributed to its having been worn by Jesus the Christ. This coat is made of a dull brown material unlike anything manufactured nowadays. It is about four feet six inches in length, the back being a trifle longer than the front; the width at the chest is twenty-seven inches, whilst at the bottom it is about three feet and a half. It is seldom that this coat is exposed to popular gaze—indeed, only three expositions have taken place during the last century : the first was in 1810, when a hundred thousand people passed through the cathedral ; the second was in 1844, when the number of pilgrims exceeded a million ; and in 1891 the number exceeded all that had formerly been known. If we glance at these numbers, it will be difficult to say that the interest in charms is on the decrease. Many cures of various diseases and afflictions

The Holy Coat of Treves and its magical properties

took place during the last exhibition.
Among these may be mentioned cases of
complete blindness, lupus, a withered
limb, St. Vitus's dance, an issue of blood,
paralysis, and intestinal tuberculosis.
These cures have of course been placed
down to imagination and suggestion ;
but this explanation is placed out of
court, when we take into consideration
the cures of children, or rather, infants
under two years of age, such as Peter Eul,
of Burdenbach.   This child of
little more than eighteen months
old is certified by Dr. Weber as
having completely lost the sight
of his right eye, owing to in-
flammation of the brain, while the sight
of the left eye had become weak, and
the right arm had become paralysed.
Medical treatment had hitherto had no
results, and any considerable improve-
ment was almost out of the question.
The child was taken to the cathedral,
and the moment it touched the charmed
coat it uttered a cry, for it is always
necessary to come into contact with this

It is not
imagination
and sugges-
tion

charm if a cure is to be performed. When they offered the child food, it grasped it with its paralysed arm, and, on returning home, they found the child could see. Two years later the doctor certified that the child could see with both eyes, and the paralysis had completely disappeared from its arm. This is only one case out of many which places the cures outside the realm of suggestion and imagination.

Under the heading of religious charms must be placed the " Holy Hand,'' or, as it is sometimes called, the " Dead Hand.'' This hand is known to have belonged to Father Edmund Arrowsmith, a Jesuit, who suffered the extreme penalty of the law at Lancaster, on August 28th, 1628. The story is that after his body was cut down the right hand was cut off, in compliance with his dying injunctions and to fulfil his promise that he would work miraculous cures on those it was brought into contact with. For many years the hand was kept at Bryn Hall ;

A dead hand with curative properties

5

then it was removed to Sir Robert Gerard's residence, Garswood Hall, and afterwards it was placed in the custody of the priest in the Catholic Chapel at Ashton-in-Maskerfield. Numerous and marvellous are the cures placed to its credit.

At one time Spedlin's Tower, which stands on the bank of the Annan, possessed a Bible which acted as a charm to keep a restless spirit in order and confine it to one portion of the building. On one occasion when the Bible was removed the spirit made such a commotion that the Bible was quickly recalled and placed in its usual position on the staircase, after this had been done the disturbance ceased.

General Kuropatkin, the famous Russian general, had in his possession a valuable ikon, or holy picture, which was supposed to have the power of protecting him in times of danger. This ikon was presented to him by the town council of St. Petersburg. It consists of six handsome paintings of saints

General Kuropatkin's holy talisman

of the Greek Church, enclosed in a magnificent gold frame. The idea is very prevalent among Russian soldiers, that it would be unwise to court danger without some talisman of this kind.

The famous stone of Caaba must be classed as a holy charm. It is a black stone, and sometimes is called the " Black Stone of Mecca.'' The faithful devoutly kiss it, and look upon it as a talisman.

The Scarab, so called from its resemblance in form to that of a beetle, was used as an amulet, and was placed over the heart of the mummy by the Egyptians, or used to replace the heart itself. They are mostly composed of a hard, yellowish or dark green stone. The Egyptians were firm believers in a future state, and thought that the scarab would help to re-unite the soul and body when the time came for the soul to again inhabit the body, which was preserved for this reason. *The sacred beetle of the Egyptians*

The subject of beads is a vast one, and many people have an idea that these were

manufactured for ornaments only, but
Beads were in Egypt they were worn as a
originally religious charm. The lotus,
charms crux, ansata, and tat of Osiris
are of this type, and were used as such.

To-day we find the Hand of Mary
and the Eye Bead of Syria used as amulets.

CHAPTER X

CHARMED WELLS AND HOLY WATER

THE well of St. Winefride, in North Wales, must be looked upon as one of the most ancient institutions of the country, for it is centuries older than Canterbury Cathedral. It is now the property of the Duke of Westminster, but is leased by the Catholic Church. Its history may be called one of the fairy-tales of the Church. It is stated how, twelve hundred years ago, in the middle of the seventh century, there lived a certain Welsh chieftain on the banks of the Dever, who had the fairest daughter in the whole

St. Wine-
fride's well
and its
charmed
water

countryside.   Her name was Guenfrewi.
Marriage had no attractions for her, and
great was the consternation of the youths
in the neighbourhood when it was whispered that she was going to bury her
beauty in the cloister.   One, named Caradoc, determined that he would not lose
the girl for want of courage and attention.
He called at her parents' house, and found
Guenfrewi all alone.   Caradoc seized the
opportunity, and offered her his heart and
his hand, but to all his pleading she
turned a deaf ear, and absolutely refused
to reconsider her decision to adopt a
monastic career.   Caradoc began to
threaten, and Guenfrewi rushed through
the open door toward the church where
her parents were hearing mass celebrated by St. Beuno.   Caradoc, who was
more fleet of foot, overtook her, and,
with a blow from his sword, severed
her head from her body.   Hearing the
commotion, her parents came on the
scene and raised a piteous cry, whereon
St. Beuno left the altar and confronted
Caradoc, who stood with dripping sword

beside his victim. Seeing what had happened, the priest cursed the murderer, and in a moment the earth opened and Caradoc was swallowed up. Taking up the severed head of Guenfrewi, St. Beuno fitted it as best he could to her shoulders and covered it over with his cloak, returning to complete the celebration of mass. When this was over he removed the covering from the corpse, when lo ! they found that a great wonder had been worked, for the maiden was alive and well ; her head had reunited to her body, and where the head of the beautiful maiden had fallen, there sprung up a well of water, which from that day to this has never ceased to flow. Guenfrewi, afterwards known as St. Winefride, entered into a religious course of life, and lived at Holy Well till St. Beuno died. She was subsequently canonised, and from that day to this remains an object of devotion. The rush of pilgrims to this charmed well is so great as to somewhat overwhelm the primitive resources

St. Beuno curses Prince Caradoc

of the little village of Holywell. The magical properties of the water cannot be doubted, and even the *Lancet* does not seek to repudiate the truth

The marvellous curative power of the well cannot be doubted

of the cures, but admits their reality, and seeks to account for them in the usual way ; but as with the Holy Coat of Treves, it will be found a difficult task to place all these cures down to imagination or suggestion.

The charmed waters of Wales do not stand alone, for what Holywell is to Britain, so is Lourdes to France, and Mugnano to Italy. The cures are ascribed to St. Winefride at the one, to the Blessed Virgin at another, and the honour given to St. Philomena at Mugnano.

We need not take a journey to the

Charmed water to be found in all Roman Catholic Churches

places mentioned to find charmed or holy water, for it is used in all Roman Catholic Churches— that is, if the priests have carried out their duty conscientiously. Originally the position of the planet Jupiter was taken into account in the blessing of holy water. It is placed at the door, and the faithful on entering dip their fingers into the water, and make with it the sign of the Cross upon their foreheads or breasts. This is done in order to drive away from them evil thoughts or feelings, and to purify them for the services in which they are about to take part. In baptism, what we may term charmed water is again used, and this not only in the above Church, but also in the Church of England.

In the Southern Church of Buddhism in the East, there is a ceremony—that of the recitation of the verses of " Paritta," —where charmed water is used. Ropes are held in the hands of the monks and connected with a large vessel of water during the time taken to recite The the sacred verses. After the Buddhists ceremony the water is distributed use water as a charm and the ropes cut into pieces, in their Church which are given away, and the people receiving a piece wear it as a charm.

CHAPTER XI

THE HORSESHOE AND SOME OLD-DAY CHARMS

THE belief in the efficacy of the horseshoe as a lucky charm is widespread, and ever since it was recognised as a horseshoe, it appears to have been accounted lucky. It may be seen used as such in any town, village, or *The horse-* hamlet throughout England ; it *shoe a uni-* is popular in the United States : *versal luck* *bringer* the belief flourishes among the Teutonic and Scandinavian races, and as far east as India. No witch is said to be able to enter a building, no evil come where a horseshoe is nailed, prongs downwards. Popular superstition has for ages endowed the metal iron with protecting powers, while the half-circle or crescent is also considered fortunate. Many are the explanations given as to why this crescent of iron, the horseshoe, was, and still is, looked upon as such a powerful charm.

One story is that the holy St. Dunstan, who is the patron saint of blacksmiths, was one day at work in his forge when Satan assailed his virtue, disguised in female beauty. St. Dunstan detected the personation, and St. Dunstan shod Satan when the Satanic courtesan was with red-hot trying to fascinate him through horseshoes. his forge window, he nipped the demon's nose with hot pincers. Again Satan tried his luck in similar disguise, but St. Dunstan tied him to the forge-rack, and shod him with red-hot horseshoes. From that day forth Satan avoids blacksmiths, and even a horseshoe strikes him or his followers with terror.

The Mohammeden says it is because of the form, which is the sacred crescent of Islam. The Cingalee use them because of the resemblance to the sacred snake, Nagendra, one of their deities. The Jew looks upon it as a symbol of the Passover, where the blood sprinkled upon the lintel and door-posts appeared in the form of an arch. The Arabs and the Tuscan peasants associate the shoe with the new moon. Here, we appear to approach very near to the true origin of the belief and why it is so frequently found on doors and entrances ; for the crescent was the symbol of the Moon goddess Diana, who was supposed to be the guardian of doors and houses. There is another explanation based on astrology, and one which is worth taking into consideration. The horse is ruled by Jupiter, so is therefore considered lucky ; and anything that has been worn by this animal becomes a charm, especially when in the form of a crescent and made of the lucky metal iron.

Why is the horseshoe lucky?

Another popular luck-bringer, and one much sought after by sailors and fishermen, is a child's caul. If hung in a cabin it is supposed to prevent the ship from sinking, and the sailor who carries one of these cannot be drowned. At the present day it is no uncommon thing to see in the advertisement columns of the daily press some one advertising for one of these cauls, or that one can be obtained at a certain address. *The sailor's mascot, a child's caul*

The hair watch-guard is still with us to-day, for human hair is thought to be a strong and powerful amulet—hence we find many forms of jewellery for the holding of hair very common. During the war between Russia and Japan, lockets and brooches containing hair were given by lovers and friends to soldiers as amulets against the bullets of the Japanese. *The belief in human hair*

Among the ancient Egyptian charms we find the "Ankh," the emblem of long life ; the "Sistrum," which protects from evil, and the "Nefer," bringing good luck and happiness.

In glancing through the works written

by some of the magicians and philosophers
of the past, we find mention of many
quaint and peculiar objects, and some of
these are used and believed in at the
present day.

One writer tells us in all sincerity how
to make a charmed comb which will
remove any headache. If the pain is
on the right side of the head, the comb
must be made from the right horn of a
ram ; if the other side, then use the left
horn.

The hare has always been looked upon
as a " mystery " animal by those who
believe in these things. The
little bone in the knee-joint of
the hind leg of a hare will
quickly cure the cramp if the
part afflicted is touched with it.

The hare and the fox are "mystery" animals

Of the fox we learn that : " A small
piece of the tongue of a fox being
moistened and made soft in vinegar, after
being dried, draweth out a thorn or any
other thing deep in the flesh by laying
it thereon.''

The heart of a kite, worn about the neck

or finger, mitigates choler, wrath, contention, and preserves the wearer from all evil effects thereof. It also stops bleeding of every kind.

Albertus Magnus says of the herb heliotropion, that if a man wrap it in a bay leaf with a wolf's tooth no one can speak an angry word to the wearer. Put under a pillow, it will bring a vision before the eyes of the man who has been robbed, and he will see the thief and all his belongings.

The heart of a toad suspended by a blue ribbon round the neck will cure the king's evil. The skin of a civet-cat, worn in battle, will protect the wearer from injury. A weasel's tail carried in the pocket will repel the attacks of savage dogs. A chameleon's tongue carried by a man, he can defy all the sharpers in the world. Moonwort is a powerful charm ; it will loosen fetters, locks, and the shoes from horses' feet. One bone of a frog will engender love, another will cause hatred.

Skins, tails, and tongues of animals

CHAPTER XII

SOME CURATIVE CHARMS

CRAMP-RINGS were much worn during the middle ages, and their use in various forms has not been discarded at this day. At one time they were blessed and used by every English Sovereign from Edward the Confessor down to Queen Mary. They were worn chiefly as a virtue against the cramp, rheumatism, or falling sickness. In 1529 Henry VIII. wished to be divorced from Catherine of Arragon. Stephen Cowley was dispatched to Rome to plead with Pope Clement to grant it. Ann Boleyn was naturally interested in the success

Cramp-rings blessed by every English Sovereign

80

of the mission, and sent several rings, with the following letter :

" Mr. Stephen,—I send you here the cramp-rings and pray you to distribute them, as she (you may assure them) will be glad to do them any pleasure which shall be in my power. And thus I make an end, praying God send you Good Health.

"Written at Greenwich, 14th day of April, 1529,

            "By your assured friend,

                  "ANN BOLLEIN.''

These cramp-rings gained their efficacy from the fact that they were made from the King's Good Friday offering of gold, and blessed with a very elaborate ceremony.

Among many of the Spanish peasants a belief exists that a candle is a charm against colds or coughs. A small box made of a piece of a peculiar bark is filled with wet earth. A candle is then taken and fixed at one side of the box. On retiring to rest the candle is lighted

Colds and coughs cured by burning candles

6

and set near the patient's bed.   When the candle is burnt out the cough will have disappeared.

In the agricultural districts of England it is a popular idea that all those who carry a raw potato in the pocket can keep off all forms of rheumatism. These are sometimes carried until it is difficult to distinguish them from a large polished pebble.

The seventh son of a seventh son is a human charm, for he possesses the charmed touch or gift of healing.   This belief is sometimes varied by being ap-The seventh son of a plied to a seventh male child seventh son in succession whether or not his has the gift of healing father has been a seventh son.

In Lupton's "Notable Things," ed. 1660, we find : "It is manifest by experience that the seventh male child by just order (never a girl or wench being born between) doth heal only with touching, through a natural gift, the king's evil, which is a special gift of God, given to kings and queens, as daily experience doth witness."

The number seven plays a great part in all magical operations ; thus we find that a certain cure for blindness is to take seven pieces of spleen from seven heifers, and use these as food which a friend must partake of.   After eating, the friend must break the plate they were served on or he himself will become blind.   Rabbi Huna gave a charm for fever, and the patient had to take seven different grapes from seven different grapevines, seven chips from seven joists, seven nails from seven bridges, seven small quantities of ashes from seven stoves, seven bits of earth from seven holes in the ground, seven pieces of pitch from seven ships, seven grains of cumin, seven hairs from an old dog.   Bind all these together and wear them over the nape of the neck.

The number seven of importance in charms

CHAPTER XIII

SPELLS, OR WRITTEN CHARMS

HERE are many forms of words and designs by means of which certain occult results are supposed to be achieved, these are usually called spells. Perhaps the most common one is the well-known word " Abracadabra," sometimes written as " Abrasadabra." This word must be written on parchment or paper, the first line in full, then the second line has the last letter **The mystic** omitted, and so on, till in the **word** last line there only remains the **" Abraca-** **dabra "** letter A, the whole forming an inverted cone. It is used for the curing of diseases. Lord Byron, who was a believer in the power of such

things and who had a knowledge of many Scotch spells, recommends this charm for the curing of ague.

Another specimen of these old spells is one to obtain favour and love. The following words are written on virgin parchment : " Sator, Arepo, Tenet, Opera, Rotas, Jah, Jah, Jah, Enam, Jah, Jah, Kether, Chokmah, Binah, Gedulah, Geburah, Tiphereth, Netzach, Hod, Yesod, Malkuth, Abraham, Isaac, Jacob, Shadrach, Meshach, Abednego, be ye all present in my aid and for whatsoever I shall desire to obtain.''

The following words engraved upon a cornelian which was taken from an ancient tomb at Cirencester are a good example :

Rotas
Opera
Tenet
Arepo
Sator.

The words may be read backwards or forwards, up and down at will.

One of the old-day charms used for good or evil contains the following verse :

" It is not this blood I wish to burn,
But . . . heart I wish to turn ;
Let them not eat, sleep, drink, nor rest
Until they come to me and do my request."

There is a spell in India named the Scorpion charm, and this is used for the treatment of scorpion bites and neuralgic pains. It is made in the form of a five-pointed star with the figure of a scorpion in the centre, the whole enclosed in a double circle in which is written the eighteenth verse of the sixteenth chapter of St. Mark.

The Scorpion charm of India for bites and neuralgia

A short inscription on paper, skin, or cloth is the most widespread form of charm known in the Eastern Countries. The writer of these charms often goes through a special course of instruction to prepare him for the work. Among these are those which will enable the wearer to discover treasure, to win the favour of a woman or man, to discover a runaway wife, to deliver a house or person from evil spirits, and even those to bring friction between husband and wife or to compass the death of an enemy. Some of these professional charm-writers have over two hundred of these spells to choose from.

It is not usually known that each Psalm of our Western Bible is a potent spell, yet this is found to be so if we read the Mosaic books of the Cabala and the Talmud. For example, of Psalm seventeen it is written that : " A traveller, who prays this psalm early in the morning, with ardour, together with the proper prayer, in the name of Jah, will be secure from all *The magical book of Psalms, all of which are spells for certain purposes* evil for twenty-four hours. The prayer is as follows : ' May it be thy holy will, O Jah, Jenora, to make my journey prosperous, to lead me in pleasant paths, to protect me from all evil, and to bring me safely back to my loved ones, for thy mighty and adorable name's sake. Amen.' "

Psalm twenty-one will give safety in storms, we read : " During an existing storm at sea, when there is danger at hand, mix rose-oil, salt, water, resin ; pronounce over it slowly this psalm, and the holy name Jehaen, and then pour the consecrated salve into the foaming sea while uttering the following prayer : ' Lord of the world, thou rulest the pride of the foaming and roaring sea, and calmest the terrible noise of the waves. May it please thee for the sake of thy most holy name, Jehaen, to calm the storm and to deliver us mercifully from this danger. Amen. Selah.' ''

In Psalm twenty-three we find a charm by which we may receive reliable instructions in regard to something through a dream or vision. The method is A Psalm to bring about to purify by fasting and bathing ; prophetic pronounce the Psalm with the dreams or visions holy name Jah seven times, and pray at the end of each repetition : "Lord of the world, notwithstanding thy unutterable might, power, exaltation and glory, thou wilt still lend a listening ear to the prayer of thy humblest creature, and wilt fulfil his desires. Hear my prayer also, loving Father, and let it be pleasing to thy most holy will to reveal unto me in a dream, whether (here the affair of which correct knowledge is desired must be plainly stated) as thou didst often reveal through dreams the fate of our forefathers. Grant me my petition for the sake of thy adorable name, Jah. Amen. Selah.''

If compelled to travel alone by night, pray the one hundred and twenty-first Psalm reverently seven times, and you will be safe from all accidents and evil occurrences. Psalm one hundred and twenty-seven written upon pure parchment, placed in a clean bag, and suspended from the neck of a newborn son immediately after birth, no evil can ever befall him.

Before entering college or under- How students can taking mental work Psalm one strengthen hundred and thirty-four should their mental powers and be repeated; it consists of have success only three verses. The division "Beth'' in the one hundred and nineteenth Psalm may also be used for the same purpose.

Other scriptural charms are Chapter 5 Job, verses 22 and 23 are good against furious beasts. Verses 19, 20, and 24 against trouble in general. For the overcoming of enemies take Isaiah, Chapter 12, verse 2 ; Chapter 13, verse 10 ; and Chapter 17, verse 14 ; while to protect from peril by fire and water Isaiah, Chapter 43, verse 2 is potent.

CHAPTER XIV

THE INDIVIDUAL, FAMILY, TRIBAL, AND NATIONAL CHARM

NDER the first heading must be placed charms outside of those handed down from one person to another, for the individual charm is of benefit to one person only, and may be one which has been found or bought because of some impression or presentiment that it would bring good luck. An example of this class will be the golden skull mentioned as belongng to Mr. Austin Osman Spare, the artist. These individual charms appear to come into

The individual charm

the life at some period, and to herald
luck or to shield from danger, and
to lose their efficacy and drop out of
history at the death of the one they
have benefited.

The family class is a large one, and
consists of those handed down from father
to son, or by one member of the family
to another, and such as appear to affect
the whole family. Here we can
The family place the toadstone ring of the
charm German Emperor, the Spanish
opal, the ring of the Napoleons,
the vase of Edenhall, and many others
given in the previous part of this
work.

Under the heading of tribal we can
include various religions, organisations,
and bodies, and though this is not so large
as the family class, yet it will
The tribal not be difficult to give some
charm example. We have the various
religious sects with their relics :
the Mohammedans with their black stone
of Mecca ; the jewels with their Caba-
listic designs of the Masons ; the gems

of the Gnostics ; the sapphire mascot of the Jews ; the totems of the many tribes of North American Indians. The tribal charm has other attributes besides bringing good luck to the people ; it has also a binding and strengthening influence, and is used for holding the tribe or body together in fraternal bonds, so that it will not be a great stretch of imagination to class the colours and standards of various regiments under this heading.

Coming to the national charm, perhaps one of the best illustrations of this type will be the Coronation stone, which may be termed the English national charm. The Jews have their ark, also Aaron's breastplate of precious stones said to be the Urim and Thummin which possessed properties of an occult nature, each stone representing one of the twelve tribes. For the Chinese we get the black stone of Mukden. For the same reason as we claimed the standards and colours as tribal charms, so under

The national charm

the national we will include the Union Jack, the Stars and Stripes, and all other flags used to inspire the many nations with patriotism and the soldiers with courage.

SECTION II

OCCULT JEWELLERY AND GEMS: WHEN, WHERE, AND HOW TO USE THESE

"A gift is as a precious stone in the eyes of him that hath it : withersoever it turneth, it prospereth."
—*Proverbs xvii 8.*

"Sweet are the uses of adversity,
Which, like a toad, ugly and venomous,
Wears yet a precious jewel in his head."
—*Shakespeare.*

"He who possesses a turquoise will always be sure of friends."—*Unknown.*

"Of Talismans and Sigils knew the power,
And careful watch'd the Planetary hour."
—*Pope.*

"Oh, mickle is the powerful grace that lies
In herbs, plants, stones, and their true qualities."
—*Unknown.*

CHAPTER XV

WHAT THE WORLD SAYS

ROM time immemorial an opinion has obtained that every gem and metal possess peculiar virtues. As there is a language of flowers, so there is also one of gems. Every stone has a power either for good or evil ; and we have seen how the important events in the lives of celebrities appear to have been in many cases connected with some class of charm.

Every gem a charm for good or evil

" Are we less superstitious than our ancestors, or are we more cautious in disclosing ourselves ? '' Such is the query one of the leading papers propounds ; it

then gives the answer by stating that,
" A glance into the fashionable jewellers
of London is sufficient to answer the
question negatively. Here is an amulet
of ancient Egyptian workmanship, a tiny
figure of Amen-Ra, or a miniature of the
god Osiris, which is supposed to bring my
' ladye fayre' luck at bridge or at Goodwin.
Little amulets, usually in the form of
dogs or horses are being worn on watch-
chains or bracelets, and ancient gems of
weird and mystic design are hung upon
slender neck-threads and tucked out of
sight, but touched on occasion to ensure
good luck to the wearer.''

A writer in *The Referee* says, " The
belief in ' mascottes ' or talismans is very
popular. Charms in the form of horseshoes, pigs, four-leaved clover,
and countless other fancies are
very general, and at present very
fashionable. I have worn a
' lucky bean ' for seven years
and never lost it. I should
very much dislike to part with it, and
have a sort of half-belief in its bringing

A "lucky bean" worn for seven years by a writer in *The Referee* me luck, or at least ' keeping off ' ill-luck.''

From another source we read : '' A fancy is now shown for wearing stones or other things which are supposed to bring good fortune. Some women wear a pendant or charm made of New Zealand jade, known as Pounamu stone. Then, others have faith in some ornament found on a mummy and worn by an Egyptian princess when the world was young. Such, for example, are the quaint jewels owned by Mrs. Clarence Mackay, or the weird cornelian necklace, given by Sir John Scott to the Hon. Mrs. St. John Brodrick at the time of her marriage. Madame Sarah Bernhardt's favourite 'mascot ' is a necklet of nuggets, given her by the miners in California ; and an English actress, Miss Irene Vanbrugh, pins her faith to a girdle of splendid uncut turquoises.''

Madame Sarah Bernhardt's favourite mascot

Under the title of '' The Present Craze for Pretty Mascots,'' another paper says, '' The jewellers have little to complain about in these days. Customers who come in and ask for tiaras that cost ten thousand pounds or so may not be as common as raindrops in February, but the number of people who buy pretty little ornaments now far exceeds those of a generation ago." Again : " The King himself has revived the popularity of gemmed horseshoe brooches by giving one set with rubies to a recent bride."

The King favours horseshoe brooches

It is also stated that the King is partial to those little charms in the shape of dogs, and has presented many of these to his friends. Miss Constance Collier, we are told, inclines to the black sweep as a mascot which brings luck. Two little wooden clogs are cherished for the same purpose by Miss Louie Freear ; and Miss Charlotte Granville believes in the efficacy of white heather as a charm, but also wears the lucky pig of green stone that hails from New Zealand. The gold heart is the fancy of Miss Beatrice Ferrar, who always wears one given by her sister for good luck.

In *Pearson'ι Weekly,* January, 1905, it is stated : "Many Society women are the proud possessors of a novel ring. With it on her finger she is sure to be lucky in love and fortunate *Pearson's Weekly on occult jewellery* in business enterprise. The gem which is appropriate to the month in which the owner was born is in the centre."

These are but a few cases culled from the daily press, and are given here to show the belief which exists at the present day in charms and amulets ; in short, the wealth of examples which can be gathered from all quarters cannot leave a doubt as to the truth of what we have previously mentioned, "that jewellery was always, and is even now, sub-consciously worn for its magic pro-perties."

CHAPTER XVI

DESCRIPTION OF STONES USED
AS CHARMS

THE following list will give some idea of the large number of stones used in occult jewellery, some of which are very rare and seldom met with. Readers will be able to classify any gems they may possess by referring to this list.

Agate.—A semi-pellucid, incrystallized variety of quartz, of which there are many kinds. The same specimen presents various tints, and the colours are delicately arranged in stripes or bands, or blended in clouds. The fortification agate or Scotch pebble, the moss-agate, and the clouded agate are familiar varieties.

Alexandrite.—A newly discovered precious stone, and so named because it was found in Russia on the birthday of the present Czar. In daylight it is green, and in artificial light red—the Russian war colours.

Amber.—A yellowish translucent resin found as a fossil in alluvial soils, or on the seashore in many places. By friction it becomes strongly electric.

Amethyst.—A variety of crystallized quartz of a purple or bluish violet colour. An Oriental Amethyst is similar to a sapphire.

Ammonite.—A fossil cephaloped shell related to the nautilus : usually dark or black, and round in shape and perforated in one or two places. Sometimes called the serpent stone.

Aquamarine.—A sea-green variety of beryl.

Beryl.—A mineral of great hardness ; there are many shades of colour, seagreen or bluish green, yellow, pink, and white.

Bezoar or Beza.—There are two kinds :

one found in India, and the other in Peru ; it is a calculous concretion found in certain animals, as the wild goat, the gazelle, and the lama.

Bloodstone.—A green siliceous stone, sprinkled with red jasper as if with blood. It is also called the heliotrope.

Brazilian Pebble.—A transparent and colourless rock crystal.

Brilliant.—A precious stone of sea-green colour, though it is applied to other gems of the finest cut, formed into faces and facets, so as to reflect and refract the light, by which it is rendered more brilliant.

Bufonite.—An old name for the toad-stone, so called because this stone is supposed to have been found in the head of a large yellow species of toad.

Carbuncle.—A beautiful gem of a rich red colour found in the East Indies. When held up to the sun it loses its deep tinge and becomes of the colour of a burning coal. Sometimes this name is applied to the ruby, sapphire, red spinel, and garnet.

Carnelian or Cornelian.—A variety of chalcedony, of a clear, deep, red flesh colour, or reddish white ; often used for seals.

Cat's Eye.—A variety of quartz or chalcedony, exhibiting opalescent reflections from within, like the eye of a cat. It is also applied to other gems affording like effects. It is sometimes termed the chrysoberyl.

Chalcedony.—Includes various varieties of quartz. It is usually of a whitish colour and a lustre like wax. The agate, onyx, carnelian, etc., are varieties of this.

Chalchihuitl.—The Mexican name for the turquoise.

Chrysoberyl.—See Cat's Eye.

Chrysolite.—Composed of silica, magnesia, and iron, of a yellow to green colour. The yellow varities of topaz and tourmaline.

Coral.—The red coral used in jewellery is the stony axis of the stem of a gorgonian.

Cornelian.—See Carnelian.

Corundum.—The earth alumina as found in a crystalline state, including sapphire, which is the fine blue variety ; the oriental ruby or red sapphire ; the oriental amethyst, or purple sapphire ; and adamantine spar, the hair brown variety. The gem varieties of the corundum have always been considered by Oriental nations as the most valuable after the diamond.

Crocidolite.—A mineral occurring in silky fibres of a lavender-blue colour. A variety of this is named the Tiger's Eye.

Crystal.—The material of quartz in crystallization, transparent or nearly so, and either colourless or slightly tinged with grey.

Diamond.—A precious stone or gem, excelling in brilliancy and beautiful play of prismatic colours, remarkable for extreme hardness. Usually colourless, but some are yellow, green, blue, and even black. They are said to be of the first water when very transparent, and of the second or third water as the transparency decreases. The rose diamond, one side of which is flat and the other cut into twenty-four triangular facets in two ranges, which form a convex face pointed at the top.

Egyptian Pebble.—A brownish yellow variety of jasper.

Emerald.—A variety of beryl of a rich green colour.

Feitsui.—The Chinese name for pale green jade.

Fire-stone.—A name given to the carbuncle.

Garnet.—This is a silicate; there are white, green, yellow brown, and black varieties. The transparent red stones used as gems are related to the carbuncle of the ancients.

Heliotrope.—See Bloodstone.

Hyacinth.—A red variety of zircon, consisting of silica and zirconia.

Jacinth.—See Hyacinth.

Jade.—A stone commonly of a pale to dark green colour, sometimes whitish. A pale green jade is the feitsui or yu-chi of the Chinese.

Jargon.—Pale yellow or smoky brown varieties of zircon.

Jasper.—An opaque variety of quartz of red, yellow, and other dull colours. When the colours are in stripes it is called striped or banded jasper. See Egyptian Pebble.

Lapis-lazuli.—An aluminous mineral of a rich blue colour, known as Armenian stone.

Malachite.—A stone usually of a concentric fibrous structure ; in colour, green or blue.

Moonstone.—A pellucid variety of feldspar, showing pearly or opaline reflections from within. The best specimens are said to come from Ceylon. It derives its name from its fancied resemblance in lustre to the moon. See Selenite.

Ojo de Buey.—A jewel-like product of nature, probably a fossil bean. In size and appearance it resembles an ox's eye.

Olivine.—A common name of the yellowish green mineral chrysolite.

Onyx.—A veined gem ; chalcedony in parallel layers of different shades of colour. It is used for making cameos, the figure being cut in one layer with the next as a ground.

Opal.—There are many varieties : they present a peculiar play of colours or delicate tints. The harquelin has a varied play of colour in a reddish ground ; the fire opal has colours like the red and yellow of flame ; common opal has a milky appearance.

Ophite.—A greenish porphyry, spotted like a serpent.

Ox's Eye.—See Ojo de Buey.

Pearl.—A shelly concretion, usually rounded and having a brilliant lustre with varying tints. Found in the shell of the pearl oyster.

Peridot.—A green variety of chrysolite.

Ruby.—A precious stone of a carmine red colour, sometimes verging into violet or intermediate between carmine and hyacinth red. It is a red crystallized variety of corundum.

Sapphire.—The blue transparent variety of corundum, usually bright blue, but in artificial light is nearly black. A new variety called the New Mine Sapphire keeps its colour at night and shines very luminously.

Sardonyx.—A variety of onyx of a reddish-yellow colour, consisting of sard and white chalcedony in alternate layers.

Scotch Pebble.—Varieties of quartz as agate, chalcedony, etc.

Selenite.—See Moonstone.

Siderite.—An indigo variety of quartz.

Snakestone.—This stone, or rather, bone, is said to be taken from the head of the cobra, and is only found in one cobra out of a great number, making that snake a king cobra. It is similar in composition to the toadstone.

Spinel.—A mineral of great hardness and various colours, as red, green, blue, brown, and black. The red variety being the spinel ruby.

Starstone.—The asteriated sapphire.

Stone-of-Memphis.—A small pebble, round, polished, and very sparkling. Dioscorides and Pliny give a full description of this famous stone.

Tiger's Eye.—A yellow-brown variety of crocidolite, similar to the cat's eye.

Toadstone.—See Bufonite.

Topaz.—A mineral occurring in rhombic prisms, generally yellow and pellucid, sometimes massive and opaque.

Topazolite.—A topaz-yellow variety of garnet.

Tourmaline.—A name given to a stone in Ceylon of which there are many shades, black is the most common, but there are also blue, red, green, brown, and white. The red and green when transparent are valued as jewels.

Turquoise.—A fine light blue colour ; a hydrous phosphate of alumina containing a little copper. Often written Turcois and Turkois. See Chalchihuitl.

Yu-Chi.—See Jade.

CHAPTER XVII

NATIONS AND THEIR FAVOURITE GEMS

SO widely spread was the belief in the mystical properties of precious stones that we find Pliny citing thirty-six writers on this subject. Nearly all nations have their favourite gem : thus opals were favoured by the Greeks, and were thought to possess great power of giving the gift of prophecy and foresight to the owner, provided he used it not for selfish gain. If he did, it became an unfortunate stone, the owner becoming unlucky in his loves and de-

Thirty-six ancient writers on the occult properties of gems

sires, and disappointment became his companion. Perhaps the modern idea of the opal being unlucky had its foundation in this Grecian belief. In ancient Mexico the opal was the most sacred of stones, and said to contain the Soul of Truth. It is the stone of the hermits, and the gem of the gods who live alone. The Mexicans claimed that it was the Soul of Fire which created worlds and men.

Among the Romans the emerald held a high place, and it was taught that a serpent would become blind if it merely looked upon an The emerald, and that every other ob- emerald valued by ject of detestation and contempt the Romans would become overwhelmed in its presence.

The Japanese commune with the Deity by gazing earnestly and intently on a large globe of pure crystal placed in the centre of the room, the family sitting around on mats with a fixed, somnolent gaze upon the stone. The answer to their petitions and desires comes through the crystal.

8

The carnelian is valued by the Shamans of Siberia and Tartary because of its magical power, through which The magic stone of Siberia and Tartary they are able to perform many wonderful feats. One of these stones, the Odem, in the breast-plate of the Jewish High Priest, possesses a great medicinal power.

The sapphire, above all other gems, is honoured by the Hindus, and is the one most frequently consecrated to their deities. A sacred occult power is ascribed to it, and the Buddhists say it will open barred doors and dwellings. It produces a desire for prayer and brings with it more peace than any other gem, but he who would wear it must lead a pure and holy life.

The Hebrews claimed the diamond as the most powerful of all gems. It is the emblem of the sun and the charm of the Invisible Fire. This stone was known to the Greeks as the Holy Necessity.

The moonstone, called by the Easterns, chandra-kanta, is said to be formed and developed under the moon's rays, this giving it occult and magical power.

If we turn to the Western Bible we shall find how important a part has been played by gems in religious symbolism. In the Book of Revelations we read of the twelve foundations of the holy city. The prophet Isaiah, among the good things promised to the Gentiles, speaks of sapphires and carbuncles. We find mention of them in Ezekiel, Job, Exodus, and many other books, while in Proverbs we read : " A gift is as a precious stone in the eyes of him that hath it : whithersoever it turneth, it prospereth.'' In the Cabala the writers specially dedicated a branch to precious stones, called Notarium, in conjunction with Lithomancy. Turning to India we have the magic necklace of Vishnu, which is made of five precious stones—namely, the pearl, ruby, emerald, sapphire, and diamond; while gems of fabulous price are found in the temples

The important part played by gems in the Western Bible

The necklace of Vishnu

and in the construction of the images throughout the country. In the great epic poem of the Ramayana, it is related how the demi-god Maha-Bali is slain, and that the different parts of his body became the germs for the various gems. From his bones came diamonds, from his eyes sapphires, from his blood rubies, from his marrow emeralds, from his flesh crystals, from his tongue corals, and from his teeth pearls.

The ruby is the sacred stone of the Burmese, who liken it to a human soul about to enter the sacred precincts of Buddha, and, consequently, in the last stage of transmigration before entering the eternal embrace of divine love.

There is rather a pretty idea about the ruby in Burmah. The natives believe that their colour changes gradually, while they ripen in the earth, like a fruit. At first, they say, the stone is colourless ; then it becomes yellow, green, blue, each in turn, the final stage

Burmah holds a curious belief about precious stones

being red. When redness is attained, the ruby is ripe. The ruby is said to influence the wearer very strongly for good or evil.

CHAPTER XVIII

THE LANGUAGE OF PRECIOUS STONES

THE following list will give the attributed virtues of those gems used for jewellery, and are those mostly worn for this purpose at the present day.

Agate.—This stone is cooling and allays fevers, quenches thirst, and quiets the pulse and heart throbs, insures good health and a long and prosperous life. They are also said by the ancients to render their wearer invisible. Bound on the horns of oxen will give a good harvest.

Amber.—Is excellent for the fires of the soul, for the eyes, and for glandular swellings of the throat and lungs. It insures the wearer good luck, and a very long enjoyment of the qualities which make the wearer attractive.

Amethyst.—This is a sure averter of drunkenness; it preserves from strong passions, and brings peace of mind; it promotes chastity, and will strengthen the will power. In battle it renders the wearer brave, far-seeing, and honourable.

Ammonite.—It is used in the religious ceremonies of the Hindus, and is said, if placed near the deathbed of one dying, to introduce his soul to the deities.

Beryl.—Used by the South Sea Islanders as a rainmaker, and said to be equally efficacious in bringing drought on their enemies.

Bezoar or Beza.—A charm against plague and poison. Tavenier, the traveller, in his works, mentions this stone, and how to tell the true from the counterfeit, he says, "There are two infallible tests: one is to place it in the mouth, and if it is genuine it will give a leap and fix itself on the palate; the other consists in placing the stone in a glass of water, and if true bezoar the water will boil.''

Bloodstone.—Gives courage, success, and wisdom in perilous undertakings. In the West Indies it is used for the cure of wounds, being wetted in cold water, and in magical works it is used in incantations. A favourite stone with the Gnostics, who employed it largely in their gems and talismans. Also called the heliotrope.

Bufonite.—Cures the bite of snakes and other poisonous reptiles.

Carbuncle.—Corrects evils resulting from mistaken friendships; it holds to the owner the passionate love of all those whose love may be desired.

Carnelian or Cornelian.—Gives content and friendship. Promotes astral vision.

Cat's Eye.—A charm against witchcraft. It is lucky and possesses the virtue of enriching the wearer. Same as the chrysoberyl.

Chrysolite.—Cures madness and despair, banishes misfortune, and gives hope.

Coral —Guards against evil. It is used

in difficulties of the heart, lungs, and in indigestion ; it excites nerve power, brilliancy and gladness, and is a true health-giver.

Crystal.—Brings calm, sweet sleep, and good dreams ; it enables the inner soul to hear the silent voice of the oracle and to foretell future events.

Diamond.—Gives faith, purity, life, joy, innocence, and repentance. Good for developing concentration and to promote spiritual ecstasy. Loses its brilliancy with the health of the wearer, and only regains it when the owner recovers. Capable of detecting poisons by exhibiting a moisture or perspiration on its surface.

Emerald.—Gives faith ; success in love, discovers false friends, promotes constancy of mind and warm, true friendship, felicity in domestic life. It changes colour when false friends or false witnesses are near, and as a love token it registers the degree of love. If it is pale, then love is waning ; if it loses colour entirely, the lover is false and the love gone for ever. Its soft green colour has a beneficial effect upon the wearer's own eyes, and is a good talisman for any eye trouble ; but serpents are said to become blind if they even look at an emerald. If worn about the neck or finger is efficacious against fits and prevents convulsions in children.

Garnet.—Constancy and fidelity in every engagement ; gives cheerfulness and the ability to hold one's own in the world. If worn out of season promotes discord between lovers.

Hyacinth.—Worn on the neck or finger will preserve the wearer from infection even if he go into an infected place ; gives honour, the support and esteem of superiors.

Jade.—A powerful bringer of luck. All Chinese have a great belief in its fortune-bestowing powers.

Jasper.—Courage, wisdom, and firmness ; success in dangerous enterprises.

Lodestone.—Will increase the mental powers, and enables the wearer to foretell future events.

Malachite.—Brilliant success and happiness in every circumstance of life.

Moonstone.—Protects from harm and danger ; very cooling in fever if applied to both temples. Good fortune in love matters.

Olivine.—Frees the mind from sadness and evil passions.

Onyx.—Disturbs the slumbers and the mind ; gives frightful dreams.

Opal.—Denotes hope and good fortune ; it sharpens the sight and strengthens the faith of the possessor. The fiery opal possesses the united virtues of all the gems into whose distinctive hues it is emblazoned : the ruby's strength and courage ; blue, the prosperity of the turquoise ; green, the emerald's faithfulness, and so with the other colours. It has long been a superstition that the opal is an unlucky stone to wear, but its original significance was good luck. It may safely be worn if it is the stone of the birth-month, or if one's birthstone is worn at the same time. If these rules are not observed, it is fatal to love and will break friendships, also the female wearing it will bear no children.

Ophite.—Gives the power to see visions and hear the voices of the invisible.

Pearl.—Gives purity and innocence, also clearness to physical and mental sight. The pearl's beauty depends much on the health of the wearer.

Peridot.—Cheers the mind, prevents irritability, and removes depression.

Ruby.—Divine power, love, dignity, and royalty. Holds to the owner the love of those loved ; corrects evils resulting from mistaken friendships ; discovers poison ; will quicken the blood and increase the will of the animal body, and will give vivacity ; will cause obstacles to melt away, and inspire with bravery and zeal. It will bring one's due in money that has been misappropriated.

Sapphire.—Truth and constancy ; denotes repentance ; frees from enchantment ; signifies piety and goodness ; insures protection against many diseases, and will warn of hidden dangers. If the possessor wears it in any haunt of dissipation his actions will at once be known to the one he holds dearest.

Sardonyx.—Gives conjugal felicity ; favours fortune. The woman whose stone it is and who neglects to wear it is doomed to a lonely existence.

Snakestone.—Renders its possessor invulnerable against the bite of snakes.

Stone-of-Memphis.—Applied to any part of the body on which it is necessary for the surgeon to operate upon it preserves that part from any pain in the operation.

Tiger's Eye.—A lucky stone ; it enriches the wearer.

Topaz.—Fidelity in friendship ; prevents bad dreams ; cheers the wearer ; strengthens the intellect ; brightens the wit ; protects against the perils of the sea ; will lose its colour in the presence of poisons ; gives nerve strength, and helps the heart and digestion.

Turquoise.—Success, happiness, and many friends ; prosperity in love, and obtains friends as is verified by the old saying : " He who possesses a turquoise will always be sure of friends." If given by a lover, it will lose its colour should the love wane, or will change colour if danger threatens the wearer.

The twelve foundations of the New Jerusalem are supposed to represent as many apostolic virtues, such as :

1. *Amethyst:* Sobriety and temperance.
2. *Beryl :* Goodness of mind at all times.
3. *Chalcedony :* Ardent zeal.
4. *Chrysolite :* Restrained by no obstacles.
5. *Chrysoprase :* Severity towards sin.
6. *Emerald :* Suavity of manner.
7. *Jasper :* Firmness and constancy
8. *Hyacinth :* Calmness in all things.
9. *Sapphire :* Heavenly and beautiful thoughts.
10. *Sardius :* Readiness for martyrdom.
11. *Sardonyx :* Variety in teaching.
12. *Topaz :* Healing power.

CHAPTER XIX

THE PLANETS AND BIRTH-MONTH STONES

CCORDING to the laws of judicial astrology, we find that each day of the week has a particular stone devoted to it; and in carrying out the correspondence of nature, we get a stone for each month, or each sign of the zodiac, and for each of the seven planets.

The gems with their equivalent signs are :

SIGN	SYMBOL	GEM
Aries	The Ram	Bloodstone
Taurus	The Bull	Sapphire
Gemini	The Twins	Emerald
Cancer	The Crab	Agate
Leo	The Lion	Ruby

SIGN	SYMBOL	GEM
Virgo ...	The Virgin ...	Sardonyx
Libra ...	The Balance ...	Chrysolite
Scorpio ...	The Scorpion ...	Opal
Sagittarius	The Archer ...	Topaz
Capricorn	The Goat	Turquoise
Aquarius...	The Water-bearer	Garnet
Pisces ...	The Fishes ...	Amethyst

The stones peculiar to the planets are as follows :

Saturn, onyx ; Jupiter, emerald and sapphire ; Mars, amethyst and blood-stone ; Mercury, agate, jade, and olivine ; Venus, turquoise and lapis-lazuli ; Sun, ruby and chrysolite ; Moon, selenite, pearl and opal.

Certain stones are lucky to every one, these are diamonds, turquoises, and emeralds; but the stone to wear for general luck is the one which is yours by right of birth. Any other stones may **How to find** be worn at the same time, but **the birth-** the birthstone should never be **month stone** given the second place and sacrificed to fashion. To ascertain the birth-gem the following table should be consulted, where it will be seen that the months are not to be taken as we have them in the almanac, but according to the sun and the zodiac and the time the sun occupies one sign. The dates to which the various gems belong are as follows :

SIGN	DURATION OF SIGN AND SUN'S PERIOD THEREIN	GEM
The Water-bearer	... Jan. 21 to Feb. 18	... Garnet
The Fishes	... Feb. 19 to Mar. 20	... Amethyst
The Ram	... Mar. 21 to April 20	... Bloodstone
The Bull ...	... April 21 to May 21	... Sapphire
The Twins	... May 22 to June 21	... Emerald
The Crab ...	... June 22 to July 23	... Agate
The Lion	... July 24 to Aug. 23	... Ruby
The Virgin	... Aug. 24 to Sep. 23	... Sardonyx
The Balance	... Sep. 24 to Oct. 23	... Chrysolite
The Scorpion	... Oct. 24 to Nov. 22	... Opal
The Archer	... Nov. 23 to Dec. 22	... Topaz
The Goat	... Dec. 23 to Jan. 20	... Turquoise

The above dates are all inclusive. If born August 26, the sardonyx will be the stone ; for April 21, the sapphire ; July 23, the agate, and so on.

It has previously been stated that Apollonius of Tyana changed his rings

daily, wearing the one with the gem
for the day.   Madame Blavatsky, perhaps
the most prominent occultist of
The days of
the week
and their
gems last century, writing in her work,
" The Secret Doctrine,'' is in
favour of this especially where a
person has to mix much in the
society of others.

The stones for the day will be :
Sunday, the ruby and chrysolite ;
Monday, the selenite, pearl, and opal ;
Tuesday, amethyst and bloodstone ; Wednesday, agate, jade, and olivine ; Thursday, emerald and sapphire ; Friday,
turquoise and lapis-lazuli ; Saturday, the
onyx.

The old magicians wore a ring which
they called the "ring of strength '' containing, as it did, the seven gems—
The " ring of
strength "
worn by
the old
magicians a ruby, emerald, selenite, amethyst, onyx, turquoise, and agate.
Those readers who wish for a
jewel of this description should
have as a centre stone their birth-gem,
which should of course hold the most
prominent position in the ring, the other

six stones may be set round this in a circle or arranged three on each side of the centre gem. " Wear it and fear no man, for thou wilt be invincible as Achilles,'' says Philadelphus.

The seven colours in heraldry have also their symbols in precious stones, namely : *Or*, topaz ; The precious *Argent*, crystal; *Sable*, diamond ; stones and their colours *Gules*, ruby ; *Azure*, sapphire ; in heraldry *Vert*, emerald; *Purpure*, amethyst.

CHAPTER XX

TALISMANIC ENGRAVED JEWELS

N this branch of our subject we approach the true science of talismans, charms, and amulets, and trespass on the fringe of practical magic. But little can be given along practical lines in a work written for the general

Engraved jewels are part of practical magic

public, for this branch must always apply to the individual, and the efficacy of the talismanic gem will depend on the time of birth and the planetary positions on the day; so that only with a knowledge of astrology can the talisman be constructed with the correct metal, gem, and design, and the right time taken for the making of it. As it is impossible to give the special talisman to each reader, we will give those names and designs which may be used for the month of birth and engraved on the birthstone or metal so as to enhance its natural magical power.

Gems are not classed as talismanic till they have passed through the engravers hands, where they are engraved and set cabalistically ; up till that time they are charms depending on their natural or artificial power. The Gnostics, Kabalists, and other occultists of the middle ages considered that this natural power of the gem was greatly enhanced by this process. *Gems in themselves are not talismans*

The Egyptians, being great believers in astrology, were accustomed to have an engraving of one of the signs of the Zodiac on some gem which was mounted as a ring. The Romans favoured engravings of certain gods and goddesses ; Venus engraved on onyx was supposed to impart strength and beauty ; Jupiter gave the necessary ambition to honours and renown ; the beryl, engraved with a frog and set in gold in the form of a pendant, is a great love talisman; the cornelian, bearing a man with a sceptre, the sardonyx, engraved with an eagle, are good for fortune ; the topaz, with a falcon, procures sympathy for its possessor ; the red coral, with a man bearing a sword, will protect the wearer from epidemics ; the onyx, inscribed with the head of a camel, will produce frightful dreams.

Very potent for good or evil are some of the geometrical designs, such as Solomon's seal, the pentacle and Solomon's pantacle, the seals of the planets, seal and magic their magic squares, the signs squares and names of the planetary spirits, and many other curious figures which are used to bring the wearer into touch with the denizens of other planes.

The appropriate metal in which to have set the birth-gem and the design or name to have engraved on the metal

or gem will be found in the following
table :

No.	BIRTH-GEM	METAL SET IN	NAME	DESIGN
1.	Garnet ...	Lead ...	Tzakmaqiel	The Water-bearer
2.	Amethyst	Tin ...	Vacabiel ...	The Fishes
3.	Bloodstone	Iron ...	Sarahiel ...	The Ram
4.	Sapphire ...	Copper	Araziel ...	The Bull
5.	Emerald ...	Platinum	Saraiel ...	The Twins
6.	Agate ...	Silver	Phakiel ...	The Crab
7.	Ruby ...	Gold ...	Seratiel ...	The Lion
8.	Sardonyx	Platinum	Schaltiel ...	The Virgin
9.	Chrysolite	Copper	Chadakiel	The Scales
10.	Opal ...	Iron ...	Sartziel ...	The Scorpion
11.	Topaz ...	Tin ...	Saritiel ...	The Horse-man
12.	Turquoise	Lead ...	Semaqiel ...	The Goat

The name or design may be engraved
alone or both if desired. The designs
may be found in any almanac, and can
easily be copied from *Zadkiels.*

The astrological symbols for the Zodiacal
signs are : Aries ♈, Taurus ♉, Gemini ♊,
Cancer ♋, Leo ♌, Virgo ♍, Libra ♎,
Scorpio ♏, Sagittarius ♐, Capricorn ♑,
Aquarius ♒, Pisces ♓. These may be
engraved in place of the other design.

Each of these engraved jewels has special rule over various affairs connected with life besides bringing good luck to those who wear them by right of birth.

More than one may be worn at the same time, but it must be remembered, as previously stated, that in all cases the birthstone must always be worn.

What may be obtained by the twelve talismanic jewels

The affairs and events they have rule over, and the class of people they should be worn by are given below. The numbers corresponding to those in first column of the foregoing table.

1. For good health, content, and to develop the psychic powers. Should be worn by the sick and depressed or those desirous of seeking into the mysteries of nature.

2. For protection from evil influences and enemies, gives dominion over the passions and animal nature. Those who wish to break the fetters of vice, or cement broken friendships, should possess this jewel.

3. For fruitfulness and propagation.

Should be worn by the newly married ; by those interested in husbandry and the breeding of animals.

4. For financial matters, and prospers all transactions and enterprises. Of value to speculators, bankers, and those dealing with money.

5. For success in travel and changes ; protects against dangers and mishaps in travel on land or water. Should be worn by sailors, commercial travellers, and all those having much activity.

6. Gives luck in connection with legacies and wills ; is helpful for the discovery of hidden treasure ; confers eloquence and enlightens the mind. Orators, actors, and those interested in mining and seeking of treasure should have this jewel.

7. Good for pleasure, hazardous risks, harmonious relations with children, success to actors, and in all love matters. Should be worn by gamblers ; those connected with the stage ; is of luck to children, to teachers, and those who seek to gain the affections of the opposite sex.

8. For health ; success to servants ; gives luck in the breeding of small animals and poultry.   Should be used by the sick ; those in subordinate positions ; breeders of dogs, cats, birds, etc.

9. For friendship, justice, marriage, or law.   Useful to those who are engaged to marry, or who are married ; to judges, lawyers, and all those seeking favour or friendship.

10. Success in warfare, contests, dangerous pursuits, and in handling medicine. Soldiers, doctors, chemists, surgeons, those entering into contests, or wherever there is risk to life should wear this.

11. Gives success to voyagers, emigrants, pioneers, and those living in foreign countries.   Should be used by adventurers, explorers, those going abroad or dealing with foreigners.

12. For honour, preferment, seeking favour, for enlightening the understanding and conferring reason.   To be worn by those seeking position or the favour of those in authority.   Politicians and rulers should possess this jewel.

It may be that there are those who would like to follow in the steps of Apollonius and change their gems daily. If so the gems given to each day *How to have a powerful talismanic jewel for each day* may be converted into potent talismans and worn on their day irrespective of birth data.

They will be as below :

Sunday.—A ruby or chrysolite set in gold, and engraved on the gem or metal a sceptred king upon a lion, or a queen with a sceptre.

Monday.—A selenite, pearl, or opal set in silver ; the design, a king riding on a doe, or a woman with a bow and arrow.

Tuesday.— An amethyst or bloodstone set in iron ; design, a king on a wolf, or a female warrior.

Wednesday.—An olivine, agate, or jade set in platinum ; design, a king riding upon a bear, or a woman spinning.

Thursday.—An emerald or sapphire set in tin ; design, a king with a javelin riding on a stag, or a woman bedecked with flowers.

Friday.—A turquoise, beryl, or lapis-lazuli set in copper ; design, a king on a camel, or a naked maiden.

Saturday.—An onyx set in lead ; design, a king, crowned and seated on a dragon, or a witch.

CHAPTER XXI

LUCKY MASCOTS AND TRINKETS

NDER this heading we wil class those trinkets sold by jewellers as luck-bringers. There are hundreds of these whose luck depends chiefly on their shape and the objects they represent. " There is quite a craze for these pretty mascots," says one writer; this *How to choose your lucky* being so, we hope to show that there may be some method in *trinkets according to* this craze and that they can be *magical law* worn according to the law of correspondence and other laws little recognised by the majority.

Among these mascots we find the model of a mummy and case, an Egyptian charm from Karnac, the Buddhist prayer-wheel, the New Zealand green-stone god, the Lincoln imp, the Mikko monkey, the lucky bean, black-sweep, gold horseshoe, the little clogs, the four-leafed clover, snakes, spiders, grasshoppers, beetles, pigs, dogs, and many others.

The Lincoln imp, the Mikko monkey, and other mascots

Many people do not rely on these trinkets, but create their own mascots ; perhaps a sudden stroke of good luck will make them cast around for the compelling cause, this may be found in having that morning picked up a peculiar stone, having received in changing money a lion shilling, a farthing, or crooked sixpence—anything a trifle out of the common may appeal to the romantic nature ; and this is then regarded as the cause, and looked to for luck in the future.

Those who place faith in these little mascots may work according to magical law by selecting their luck-bringers from the table here given :

BIRTHDAY	NAME OF MASCOT TO BE WORN
Jan. 21 to Feb. 18, or Dec. 23 to Jan. 20.	The sweep, mummy and case, the monk, Lincoln imp, skull, the elephant, ass, mouse, mole, pig, tortoise, frog, owl, crow, bat, eel, beetle.
Feb. 19 to Mar. 20, or Nov. 23 to Dec. 22.	The Buddhist prayer-wheel, the clog, ivy-leaf, almond, acorn, bean, coins, horse-shoe, horse, stag, unicorn, bee, eagle, dolphin, the fish.
Mar. 21 to April 20, or Oct. 24 to Nov. 22	The soldier, smith, arrow, mailed fist, dagger, sword, pistol, bomb, ram, dog, wolf, tiger, weasel, hawk, falcon.
April 21 to May 21, or Sep. 24 to Oct. 23	The dancer, scales, figure of Justice, the mask, Cupid, lover's knot, the two hearts, the clasped hands, the bull, swan, dove, and pigeon.
May 22 to June 21, or Aug. 24 to Sep. 23	The motor-car, the windmill, the juggler, winged Mercury, book, racquet, serpent, fox, squirrel, Mikko monkey, cat, spider, parrot, jay.
June 22 to July 23	The ship, compass, spade, anchor, sailor, diver, shell, crab, lobster, duck, water-hen, otter, chameleon.
July 24 to Aug. 23	The heart, dice, ace, crown, playing-card, sceptre, jockey, lion, cock, phœnix.

CHAPTER XXII

HOW TO WEAR CHARMS AND TALISMANS

T one time for people to wear amulets, charms, or talismanic jewellery openly was to lay themselves open to charges of witchcraft, so it was an art of the goldsmith to disguise jewellery into innocent semblance. The incantation ring was often a perfectly plain gold **At one time a crime to wear talismanic jewellery** ring set with two gems, and on pressing these stones a spring opened and disclosed the surface beneath, inscribed with mystical signs and the names of the spirits. To-day it is not considered a crime to wear these

things, so many are worn openly, as pendants, brooches, pins, some attached to bangles, watch-chains, and neckthreads ; yet even now many are worn secretly especially among men, and though it is not uncommon to see men with bangles on their wrists, yet more are worn above the elbow-joint, for there are many who are desirous to avoid being branded as superstitious.   It is stated that the wearing of bangles is a common practice with almost all the crowned heads of the world.

To those of either sex who desire to wear any charm secretly, the correct method is to have it placed in a small black silk bag and suspended from the neck by a thin red silk cord, so that it hangs on the breast or under the left arm.   Another method is *The correct method of wearing a secret charm* to have it attached to a bangle and worn above the elbow. With written spells it is an easy matter to have them placed in a piece of jewellery such as a locket, brooch, or ring.

When the charm takes the form of a

10

pretty piece of jewellery, it is hard and almost seems a crime to hide it away from the sight of others, though the ancients were very emphatic in stating that no person should be allowed to handle or see the talisman or charm of another.

A charm should be used intelligently, and where luck or success are sought after the wearer must do his part and not leave it to the charm to bring about the results alone. A charm or gem is not only useful for success in material things, but may be used to develop the spiritual side of the nature. Hold it between the finger and thumb and gaze at it steadily, or if in the dark simply hold it. Concentrate your thoughts on your highest ideal, and contemplate faithfully the conditions which you desire. A few minutes spent every day in such quiet meditation will put you in tune with the infinite and give the wearer faith, strength, and courage.

The charm as an aid to spirituality

SECTION III

THEIR EFFICACY : ANCIENT AND MODERN THEORIES

"Thus measuring things in heav'n by things on earth
At thy request, and that thou may'st beware,
By what is past, to thee I have reveal'd
What might have else to human race be hid."
—*Milton.*

"Ye spirits of the unbounded universe!
Ye who do compass earth about, and dwel
In subtler essence;
I call upon ye by the written charm,
Which gives me power over you—Rise! Appear!"
—*Unknown.*

"An active principle subsists
In all things, in all natures, in the stars
Of azure heaven, the unending clouds,
In flower and tree, in every pebbly stone
That paves the brooks, the stationery rocks,
The moving waters, and the invisible air."

"Whate'er in nature is thine own,
Floating in air or pent in stone,
Shall rive the hills and swim the sea,
And, like thy shadow, follow thee."
—*Emerson.*

CHAPTER XXIII

MAGIC

T will now be necessary to make a short study of magic, if we desire anything like a reasonable explanation as to the power behind and manifesting through charms and kindred objects. It may be that the world has risen superior to such " superstitions " but before taking it for granted that superstition and magic are the same thing, and that the theories of the old philosophers are not suited for the present age, it will be well to read what Prof. E. B. Tyler writes on Magic in the "Encyclopædia Britannica." He says, " From age to age whole branches of what was magic passed into

the realm of science.'' If this is so, then if we trace the analogy back to first principles there is no magic, and this name is only another name for science, or the name of a scientific fact before it is understood. Perhaps if we take some of the writings of the old magicians and philosophers, we may find that their explanations dressed in modern language by our professors and scientists pass as scientific theories.

The magic of yesterday may be the science of to-morrow

Cornelius Agrippa, writing on magic, says, '' Magick is a faculty of wonderful virtue, full of most high mysteries, containing the most profound contemplation of most secret things, together with the nature, power, quality, substance, and virtues thereof, as also the knowledge of whole nature; and it doth instruct us concerning the differing and agreement of things amongst themselves, whence it produceth its wonderful effects, by uniting the virtues of things the application of them one to the other, and to their

The great magician Cornelius Agrippa and his definition of magic

inferior suitable subjects, joining and knitting them together thoroughly by the powers and virtues of the superior bodies. This is the most perfect and chief science, that sacred and sublimer kind of philosophy, and, lastly, the most absolute perfection of all most excellent philosophy. For, seeing that all regulative Philosophy is divided into Natural, Mathematical, and Theological, Natural Philosophy teacheth the nature of those things which are in the world, searching and enquiring into their Causes, Effects, Times, Places, Fashions, Events, their Whole and Parts ; also

The Number and the Nature of those things
Call'd Elements, what Fire, Earth, Air forth brings,
From whence the Heavens their beginnings had,
Whence Tide, whence Rainbow in gay colours clad.
What, makes the Clouds that gathered are, and black,
To send forth Lightnings, and a Thundering crack;
What doth the Nightly Flames, and Comets make;
What makes the Earth to swell, and then to quake;
What is the seed of Metals, and of Gold,
What Virtues, Wealth, doth Nature's Coffer hold.

All these things doth Natural Philosophy the viewer of Nature, contain.''

Again, he writes, '' Now Theological

Philosophy or divinity teacheth what God is, what the mind, what the intelligence, what an angel, what a devil, what the soul, what religion, what sacred institutions, rites, temples, observations, and sacred mysteries are. It instructs us also concerning faith, miracles, the virtues of words and figures, the secret operations and mysteries of seals ; and, as Apuleius saith, it teacheth us rightly to understand, and to be skilled in the ceremonial laws, the equity of holy things, and rule of religions. . . . . Pythagoras, Empedocles, Democritus, Plato, and many other renowned philosophers travelled far by sea to learn this art; and being returned, published it with wonderful devoutness, esteeming of it as a great secret. Also it is well known that Pythagoras and Plato went to the Prophets of Memphis to learn it, and travelled through almost all Syria, Egypt, Judea, and the schools of the Chaldeans, that they might not be ignorant of

Magic teaches the secret and mysteries of seals

Pythagoras and Plato travelled far to learn the occult secrets

the most sacred memorials and records of magick, as also that they might be furnished with divine things. Whosoever, therefore, is desirous to study in this faculty, if he be not skilled in Natural Philosophy, wherein are discovered the qualities of things, and in which are found the occult properties of every being, and if he be not skilful in the mathematics, and in the aspects and figures of the stars, upon which depend the sublime virtue and property of everything, and if he be not learned in theology, wherein are manifested those immaterial substances which dispense and minister all things, he cannot be possibly able to understand the rationality of magick. For there is no work that is done by mere magick, nor any work that is merely magical, that doth not comprehend these three faculties.''

It will thus be seen that magic is a high system and state of knowledge in both philosophy and science. At an early period it was divided into four classes. These were : 1st, Natural Magic ; 2nd,

The four classes of magic

White Magic ; 3rd, Black Magic ; 4th, Divine Magic. We need only touch that class to which our subject belongs, and that is chiefly the first, or Natural Magic, where we are brought into connection with the spiritual world through artificial or natural agents.

CHAPTER XXIV

ANCIENT OCCULT THEORIES

T is well known by students of the occult that spirit does not act immediately upon matter ; there must always be a medium between them. Spirit and matter are the two poles of one and the same substance needing an intermediate middle as a point The indispensable of conjunction and exchange agent of of energy. Seeing this, then, every magical performance it may not be inappropriate to suggest that this medium is that invisible, mysterious something in which the matter atoms float, called by the Hindus, Akasa ; by the Hermetic

philosophers, Azoth ; by the Occultists and Magicians, Astral Light, or Anima Mundi ; by the Rosicrucians, the Universal Fire ; and by Modern Scientists, Luminiferous Ether. It is the indispensable agent of every magical performance, religious or profane. It permeates all things, going through flesh and blood, steel and glass, the diamond and sapphire, with the facility of water through a net. It is the link between all things, between the stars and the human body, between plants and minerals, and is the media by means of which all our spiritual efforts can be exerted upon nature. Through **The secret** it each body may produce **of affinities** **and anti-** certain changes in the activity **pathies** of life in another body that is in sympathy with the former ; on it rests the whole teaching of affinities and antipathies.

We have quoted Agrippa on Magic, and will now see what he has to say on this medium. He writes as follows : " The ever-changing universal force, the ' soul of the world,' can fecundate anything by infusing in it its own celestial properties. Arranged according to the formula taught by science, these objects receive the gift of communicating to us their virtue. It is sufficient to wear them to feel them immediately operating on the soul as on the body.''

Paracelsus, one of the most learned philosophers and mystics, says, '' The sun and the stars attract something from us and we attract something from them, because our astral bodies are in sympathy with the stars, and the stars are in sympathy with our astral bodies ; but the same is the case with the astral bodies of all other objects. They all attract astral influences from the stars. Each body attracts certain particular influences from them : some attract more, others less ; and on this truth is based the power of amulets and talismans and the influences which they may exercise over the astral form of the bearer. Talismans are like boxes in which sidereal influences may be preserved.''

Paracelsus on the nature of talismans

Again, he says, " There are certain stars whose influence corresponds to the medical qualities of certain metals, and others that correspond to those of certain plants, and they may act for good or for evil if they are attracted by corresponding elements in the sidereal body of man. If, for instance, a woman is deficient in the element whose essence radiates from Mars, and consequently suffers **How Mars** from poverty of blood and want **acts upon** **the human** of nervous strength, anæmia, **body** we may give her iron, because the astral elements of iron correspond to the astral elements contained in Mars, and will attract them as a magnet attracts iron.''

Dr. Hufelans, in a work on Magic, profounds the theory of the universal magnetic sympathy between men, animals, plants, and minerals, and confirms the testimony of Campanella, Van Helmont, and Servius, as to the sympathy existing between the different parts of the body as well as between the parts of all organic and even inorganic bodies.

In an old work on Magic it is stated,
" In the grand laboratory of nature there
are many singular compositions of herbs
and minerals, which have a surprising
effect in themselves without the least
assistance from supernatural agency ; for
in the commixture of bodies of a similar
nature, there is a twofold power and
virtue, first when the celestial
properties are duly disposed in The occult
any natural substance, then affinity of
natural
under one form divers influences things
among
of superior powers are com- themselves
bined; and, secondly, when from
artificial mixtures and compositions of
natural things, combined amongst themselves in a due and harmonical proportion,
they agree with the quality and force of
the heavens under certain correspondent
constellations. This proceeds from the
occult affinity of natural things among
themselves.''

In 1643 Father Kircher, a monk, wrote
several works on Magic, wherein he
stated that a needle can be magnetised
by simply being held in the hand of a

strong-willed man ; so that man can impart his own life, and, to a certain degree, animate inorganic objects.

Coming to the end of last century, we find Madame H. P. Blavatsky refers frequently to this force in her works, " Isis Unveiled,'' and " The Secret Doctrine.'' She writes, " The occult power of plants, animals, and minerals, magically sympathise with the superior natures, and the divine soul of man is in perfect intelligence with these inferior ones.''

Speaking of magic, she says, "The corner-stone of magic is an intimate practical knowledge of magnetism and electricity : their qualities, correlations, and potencies. Especially necessary is a familiarity with their effects in and upon the animal kingdom and man. There are occult properties in many other minerals equally strange with that in the lodestone, which all practitioners of magic must know, and of which so-called exact science is wholly ignorant. . . . One common vital principle pervades all things,

The corner-stone of magic

and this is controllable by the perfected human will.''

From the foregoing it will be seen that the ancients were familiar with a force to which they gave various names—a universal force, which is the link between man and nature. A universal force which is the link between man and nature They were also aware that, though this force interpenetrates all space, it gathers more thickly or becomes more dense around certain centres, such as the brain of man, the heart, the spine, the roots of flowers, and the seeds of minerals. It was a specialisation of this force which was the " luminous sphere " of Paracelsus ; on it Mesmer based his theory of " Animal Magnetism " ; while it was the " Od " and " Odylic Fluid " of Reichenbach, for this force manifests in many conditions.

CHAPTER XXV

MODERN SCIENCE AND OCCULT
THEORIES

THOSE interested in mysticism who are living at the present day, find themselves in the position where they are able to prove those words of Prof. E. B. Tyler, which were previously quoted, that, "From age to age whole branches of what was magic passed into the realm of science." The magic of the ancients is still with us ;

Ancient magic is still with us

for through the far past and on to the present century, it has flowed down through many channels, these usually being the various occult lodges and societies whose work it was to keep alive this knowledge, and the "discoveries" and lines of investigation pursued by our modern scientists have justified many of the statements made in the past by these ancient magicians, and handed on to the trained scientist of to-day by the modern occultist. It is not difficult to recognise the ether of our scientists as the universal force of the ancients, akasha, and just as readily may be seen in what is termed the compounds of modern chemistry the elements of the old alchemists.

In its new dress of hypnotism we find the force spoken of by Father Kircher, the Animal Magnetism of Mesmer, and the Mesmerism of Dr. Esdail, and many others. The N-rays of R. Blondlot, the Human Radiations of M. Tessier d'Helbaicy, and those mentioned by Prof. Charpentier and others, are but other names for the "luminous sphere," "od," "odylic fluid," and "aura" of those occult writers and investigators, Paracelsus, Baron Reichen-

The N-rays of Blondlot are but the aura of the old occultists

bach, Madame Blavatsky, Dr. Hartmann,
C. W. Leadbeater, J. C. F. Grumbine, and
W. J. Colville.

R. Blondlot says that all objects store
up and radiate what he terms these
N-rays; ancient and modern occultists
tell us that everything organic or inorganic has its astral counterpart, which
penetrates and surrounds it. Reichenbach spoke of a mysterious kind of light
emanating from crystals, magnets, and
from human finger-tips.

Our latest discoveries go to prove that
these various rays are of great curative
power, that human rays or emanations
can be manipulated by the human will
and given the power of evil
Human rays or good, so that they may be
can be
manipulated made poisonous or vitalising
by the
human will by the thought of the person
emitting them. Experiments
have been tried on plant-life, two plants
of the same age, and both in a healthy
condition, are subjected to these human
rays, one is treated with affection and
willed mentally to grow to perfection, the

other, though cared for and watered at the same time, and having the same surroundings, does not receive the mental affection and good thoughts, but is cursed and thoughts of hate sent out to it. The result is, that in two or three weeks the cursed plant begins to wither, while the other grows healthy and strong. What is this but the witchcraft of the middle ages ? Is it not akin to the " evil eye," so much believed in at the present day in Italy ? In the experiment given the victim is a plant, in witchcraft and with the " evil eye," it is an animal or a human being.

Witchcraft and the evil eye

All magnetic healers are aware that in treating a patient they actually draw something away from the person, and if not careful will themselves take on the aches, pains, or disease which they have rid their patients of.

CHAPTER XXVI

NATURE SPIRITS: THE POWER
BEHIND THE GEM

IT has been shown that both ancient and modern scientists are at one in a belief in a general principle of nature to which they have given various names ; and though this has cleared our ground in some measure, there is yet another fact in nature to examine before our theory as to the efficacy of charms, especi-

Nature spirits guide all natural forces ally gems, can be made clear. And here we find a difference between the science of the ancients and of the moderns. Modern scientists have not yet " discovered " those living intelligences which

function through and guide all natural
forces ; so far they have not accepted
from that middle man, the present day
occultist, this truth handed to him by
the past grand masters of magic.

We are told that humanity only plays
a small part in nature, that there are other
evolutions beside ours, and that each
kingdom of nature has its inhabitants, and
though these may be invisible to us,
nevertheless they exist and play a great
part in the evolution of the universe.
They are called Natural Elementals, or
Nature Spirits, and those we have to take
into account in our subject are divided
into five main classes ; they are the
creatures evolved in the kingdoms of
ether, fire, air, water, and earth.
Readers of mythology may The inhabi-
recognise them in the pixies, ether, fire,
fairies, elves, and brownies. air, water,
They are distinct creations, and
it is seldom they make themselves
visible to man, being engaged in the
carrying out of the activities connected
with their own elements, for they are the

powers of nature, and do what is usually ascribed to her. In the Kabala we find these creatures as ministering everywhere from the Zodiac down to the smallest worm. It is stated that there is not a thing in the world, not the least herb over which is not set a spirit, for it

A spirit guides the growth of every herb

is these which are concerned in the building of the various forms of minerals, plants, and animals, also in the building of the human physical body. Their bodies are formed of a rarer class of matter than the human physical body, thus their invisibility. Among them is found different grades of unintelligence, as in humanity. By understanding their nature or knowing the methods of their control, as the old magicians did, they can be made to render service.

Comte de Gabalis says, " When you shall be numbered among the children of the philosophers, and when your eyes shall have been strengthened by the use of the most sacred medicine, you will learn that the elements are inhabited by creatures of a singular perfection, from the knowledge of, and communication with, whom the sin of Adam has deprived his most wretched posterity. Yon vast space stretching between earth and heaven has far nobler dwellers than the birds and gnats ; these wide seas hold other guests than the whales and dolphins ; the depths of the earth are not reserved for the moles alone ; and that element of fire, which is nobler than all the rest, was not created to remain void and useless.''

No part in space uninhabited

Ages ago these elementals were classified and names and sigilla were used to express these forces ; so powerful were they considered that it was thought to be dangerous to utter these names in certain places at certain times and seasons, for at particular configurations of the planets they were said to have great power.

Dangerous to utter their names in certain places

CHAPTER XXVII

CLASSIFICATION OF CHARMS

THIS is a difficult matter for the forces at work, though sometimes distinct will often unite and work in conjunction.

Let us first glance at what we will term artificial charms, these appear to owe their efficacy to some outside influence, usually the human will or thought, and **Artificial charms** this may be brought about consciously or unconsciously. Under this heading we will class those charms, such as religious relics and images. These have been converted into such and strengthened in their power by every devotee ; and though in most cases this has been done unconsciously, yet they have become soaked with human magnetism of a devotional nature, so that the relic or image has become, as Colonel Olcott terms it, a " psychic dynamo.'' Another type of artificial charm, though consciously made so, is holy water which has been mag- Religious netised by the priests with a relics are psychic definite object ; for water easily dynamos takes on the magnetism of any one, and a sensitive individual can distinguish between water which has been magnetised, and that which has not. Holy water impregnated by the good thoughts of a man is highly charged with magnetism and very potent for good. In the same way any object, whether valuable or worthless, may be converted into an artificial charm for good or evil. If charged by some one of trained will and one having a knowledge of the forces brought into play, the power will remain in the object for a long period, and if it is made to radiate at the same rate of vibration as that of the maker, it can be made a channel for his good or evil influence.

Mr. Leadbeater says that some of the amulets and talismans in the British Museum even retain their magical power now.

Powerful talismans in the British Museum

All objects worn by people take on their magnetism and become tuned to their rate of vibration, these may be termed artificial charms, some objects taking this on more than others, thus their chief power will have much to do with the character of the wearer. This is the reason why something worn by a lucky man is eagerly sought for, and will in a certain measure help to bring luck to its new owner ; much depends on whether the former owner or the present one's vibrations are the stronger, or, in other words, whether the charm's vibrations are stronger than the new owner's, for the stronger will tune the weaker to its vibration. The same applies to those

Whether you tune the charm, or the charm tunes you

things worn by the unlucky, or by the good or evil. Those worn by the evil take on the low vibrations of the evil person, those worn by the good and pure take on the high vibrations, and will help to fructify the germ of good or evil in any one who may wear them. Their strength depends on the individuality of their former owner, and whether he was an ordinary or an extraordinary personage.

It is not wise to wear the cast-off clothing of others, unless the character of their previous wearer is well known. *It is dangerous to wear second-hand goods*

Natural charms may be said to owe their power to both outside and inside influences. To this class belong all virgin metals, minerals, stones, and most plants and animals. They appear to possess a magical power of their own, and probably they owe this to the elements of which they are composed, and to the nature spirits ensouling or watching over their growth. Their efficacy depends chiefly on the sym- *Natural charms* pathy existing between them and the wearer or possessor, thus we find that certain stones are of value to one individual and not another ; the same with plants and herbs, as witnessed in curative work. For this reason it is recommended that the gem belonging to a person by right of birth should be worn. The various gems have each their own natural rate of vibration, and that of the ruby The natural differs from that of the turquoise, rate of vibration of and so with all. This law of precious sympathy and antipathy is the stones reason why gems lose their brilliancy with the health of the wearer ; and in the case of the ruby it is said to change colour when misfortune threatens its wearer. At the present day medical men recognise the natural curative vibrations of amber, and recommend its being worn as a charm against certain ailments.

Magical charms will be our next class, where we have the natural power of a charm greatly enhanced by the human will consciously directed for this purpose. The knowledge of the various rates of vibration and the law of correspondence with the ability to apply it, makes of that man a practical magician, hence the name of magical charm. Any gem or metal whose natural virtue has been strengthened by such a man will have great power either for good or evil. If the gems of Solomon and of the Jews are to be accredited, they would belong to this class.   **Magical charms**

Closely related to the magical charm is talismanic jewellery, talismans, and written spells. Though related there is a difference between charms and talismans, and the talismanic jewellery would appear to bridge this. While a charm may be anything from a worthless piece of fabric to a precious stone or even man, the talisman is more or less an artificial production, which may be constructed of metal, stone, or parchment, depending for its efficacy on the binding of or constraining of the elementary powers to aid the behests of the possessor.   **Talismanic jewellery, talismans, and spells**

This is done by preparing them at certain times and by observing many singular forms and ceremonies. We have

The binding of the elementary powers mentioned that the forces behind nature are intelligent, and when we add that they have many grades and classes from comparatively insignificant lives to the super-mundane orders, and that these are at the back of real talismanic magic it will be seen that the forces worked with are not to be scoffed at.

Writing of these forces, Baron du Potet, says, "How did I come to find out that art? Where did I learn it? In my thoughts? No! it is nature herself who discovered me the secret. And how? By producing before my

Baron du Potet says these forces choose friends and understand traced signs own eyes, without waiting for me to search for them, indisputable facts of sorcery and magic. And what is it determines these attractions, these sudden impulses, these raving epidemics, antipathies, and crises, these convulsions which one can make durable?

What if not the very principle we employ, the agent so decidedly well known to the ancients ? What you call nervous fluid or magnetism, the men of old called occult force. . . . An element existing in nature, unknown to most men, gets hold of a person and withers and breaks him down as the fearful hurricane does a bulrush. It scatters men far away ; it strikes them in a thousand places at the same time without their perceiving the invisible foe, or being able to protect themselves. All this is demonstrated. But that this element should choose friends and select favourites, obey their thoughts, answer to the human voice, and understand the meaning of traced signs— that is what people cannot realise and what their reason rejects, and that is what I saw ; and I say it here most emphatically, that for me it is a truth and a fact demonstrated for ever.''

Every force in nature is expressible by a formula or similitude, by the operation and expression of which it may be aroused to action. Iamblichus says, '' The

Theurgist, through the power of arcane signatures, commands mundane nature ;

The occult power of numbers and geometrical forms
no longer as man, nor as employing a human soul, but as existing superior to them in the order of the gods, he makes use of greater mandates than pertain to himself, so far as he is human.'' For this reason the magical properties of numbers and of geometrical forms are relied upon by the true magician, who knows that they are expressive of certain active principles in nature, and he therefore uses them to bring these principles into operation. The engraved gems of the Gnostics and all talismanic jewellery must be placed in this division, while all talismans, magical squares, phylacteries, and those charms depending for their efficacy on traced signs, must also be included in this class.

There is another form of charm to which we will give the name of obsessed charm, as this depends for its power on some entity, often a human disembodied one, attaching itself to the object which forms the charm. Such are most of the skulls, and those things to which the haunting of houses are placed. Weapons which have been used for crime are some- times obsessed by the spirit of the doer of the crime, and perhaps this is the reason why most of these weapons are destroyed. The mummy-case men- tioned in another part of this work would also come under this heading.

The obsessed charm

CHAPTER XXVIII

GEMS: WHENCE THEIR EFFICACY

AVING given precious stones a prominent place among charms, it may be as well to devote a few pages to them alone, giving various theories as to whence they derive their efficacy. Almost all philosophers have sought to find the reason why a certain gem will help a particular individual, and many have been the explanations given.

Pythagoras said that all things have a soul, and in the hidden subliminal self, concealed in the soul of the stone, their virtue would be found. That when a man gazed upon a stone whose soul was in affinity with his own, it threw out certain

The soul of the gem

radiations that charmed him as a serpent may charm a bird.

Aristotle says, " The virtue in stones is in the heat and cold. The heat induces form, the form subsists in the aqueous part.'' Hermes taught that all power was due to planetary causes, that virtue of things below must come from things above. Albertus Magus asserted that all power lay in form.

Another writer states that the stone is a family of mineral egos. Theophrastus held that all metals were of water, but the precious stone of earth. Plato believed that they held a sort of personality that infused its virtue into them. Democritus said, " All things are full of gods.'' Reichenbach states that, " Every crystal, natural or artificial, exerts a specific action on the animal nerve ; feeble in health, powerful in weakness.'' Jacob Bœhme declared that precious stones had their origin in the flash of light caused by love. He calls them the eye of the natural world. Other writers hold that certain lower intelligences belong to different gems, and when their owner calls upon them they obey.

These old-day ideas will hardly satisfy the scientific mind, so we will see if modern science has anything to give on precious stones which will help us to discover their power. Modern theories trace the genesis of gems to the early workings of fire and water, through which our planet has passed in the far past ages, while most agree that their constituent atoms must have been at one time in either the liquid or gaseous state ; and scientists may be divided into two classes, one holding the aqueous, and the other the igneous theory. As to the colouring matter of gems, most are agreed that this consists of various metallic oxides, though iron appears to play a prominent part in this matter, but it depends on the amount of oxygen and certain combinations as to the colour given. Hauy says there are exceptions, and some gems owe their colour to other metals.

The genesis of gems

Glancing at their electrical capacity, we find that nearly all precious stones possess this quality in varying degrees, being either positive or negative. Amoretti's investigations of the electric polarity of precious stones shows that the diamond, the garnet and amethyst are negative, while the sapphire is positive. Experiments have shown the tourmaline is positive at its one end and negative at the other—a feature which the topaz is also said to possess.

The electrical poles of precious stones

We have here sufficient to enable us to establish a theory whereby we can show how precious stones may be related to human beings ; for if the colour of the gem depends on iron, then it is well to remember that we have two principal forms of iron in the human blood, viz., protoxide of iron and peroxide of iron, a compound of the two constitutes what was formerly known as lodestone, or black magnetic oxide of iron. Perhaps science may find that certain gems

A physical affinity between man and precious stones

are tuned to the human body through vibrations generated by this magnetic principle. At any rate there must be some degree of affinity between the gem and the man so tuned, therefore we have established a physical relationship.

For any other affinity we must look to the nature spirits or elementals previously mentioned, as these can be said to be related to one of the kingdoms, *i.e.,* fire, air, earth, or water, on the one hand, and to one of the four temperaments on the other, the temperament depending on the element which **The secret of luck** predominates in the body or the nature of the man ; for man is composed of all elements, and the element which predominates in his constitution at birth will be the ruling element throughout life, and all things of like element will be in sympathy with him. This is the secret of what we term "luck." Here we find the reason why some people are lucky in one thing and not in another. Those with the earth, or gnomic element, having preponderance are lucky with metals and earthy matters ; those with the fire element strong find their luck with fire or in occupations having to do with this, and so on. If people had a knowledge of the law of correspondence, and realised that they have as their heritage a certain gem, metal, and colour, and if this knowledge were applied, then we should hear of fewer unlucky people.

A gem, metal, colour as your heritage

We have seen how our scientists are divided as to the origin and nature of gems—some leaning to fire, others to water. Probably both sides have a little of the truth. May not all the elements have their representatives in the mineral kingdom and among precious stones, as is suggested by the Easterns in the story of the magic necklace of Vishnu ?

As far evolved as man may be he is only near the centre, or standing midway between the planets with their gods and the minerals with their elementals ; yet is he linked equally to both, for all things, from the highest to the lowest, are like beads on a thread, and this thread is one of the rays of the seven planets. The ray on which a man is strung on depends on what planet had chief rule at the time of his birth. If it was Mars, then will he be tuned to all things of the Mars' nature.

Man stands midway between the planetary gods and the gem elementals

The root of all is One or the Absolute ; and from this impersonal principle emanates the rays. The ray which is guided by the great planetary spirit of Mars is tuned to the vibrations of this planet, and passes through the various orders of spirits and highly evolved beings until it reaches man, and so on, down through the animal, vegetable, mineral, and lower kingdoms—a magnetic ladder from the mineral to the gods. All things, from the lowest to the highest, which are tuned to this ray, must be in close affinity one with the other. In this way we find that each planet has its representatives on every plane and in every kingdom of nature.

A ladder from the mineral to the gods

When the earth was in its making these rays went forth upon their mission, and falling upon an aggregate of atoms in process of crystallization, the vibrations of the ray were caught and fastened in the rock or precious stone, there to lie latent until roused into activity by vibrations of a like nature playing upon them. We find a similar law at work in coal where the sun's energy or vibrations lie hidden to be set free by other heat vibrations. May it not be that the vibration of a human will, keyed to the same ray as the precious stone, can call into action the hidden virtue and ensouling elemental of that stone?

Each gem is the emblem of one of the seven great planetary hierarchies; each individual belongs unalterably to a certain hierarchy, and will Man's place have the peculiar conditions of in the that one within himself as the universe guiding principle, and to which vibrations he will be tuned. Each hierarchy has its special work, and though apparently differing in their method, yet each is filling a part of the divine thought :

> " All are but parts of one stupendous whole,
> Whose body nature is, and God the Soul."
> —*Pope.*

INDEX

Aaron's Breast-plate, 60, 93
Abbey of Scone, 32
"Abracadabra," 84
Abraham, The Precious Stone of, 59
Affinities and Antipathies, 156, 174
Agate, 102, 118, 127, 137, 139
Agrippa, Cornelius, 19, 150, 156
Akasa, 155
Alba, Duchess of, 38
Alexandra, Queen, 20
Alexandrite, 103
Alfonso XII., 8
Almudena, Virgin of, 10
Amber, 56, 103, 118
Amen-Ra, Priestess of, 52, 98
Amethyst, 103, 119, 126, 128, 131, 136, 139
Ammonite, 103, 119
Amoretti's Investigations, 183
Amulet, 56, 68, 77, 98, 172
Ancient Egyptian Charms, 77

Anecdotes, 5, 6, 10-17, 19, 20, 22, 24, 26-28, 30-33, 38, 39, 42, 43, 44, 47-50, 52-58, 63-69, 74, 75, 81, 82, 116
Angel's Written Charm, 62
Anima Mundi, 156
Animals, 49, 50, 78, 79, 83
"Ankh," 77
Anthropological Society, 3
Apollonius of Tyana, 5
Aquamarine, 103
Aquarius, The Sign, 128
Arabs, 30
Arc, Joan of, 40
Aries, The Sign, 127
Arrowsmith, Father, 65
Astrological Symbols, 135
Astrology, 76, 127, 133
Aura, 163
Azoth, 156

Baber, Founder of Mogul Dynasty, 19
Bacon, Lord, 57

Bancroft, Lady, as a Mascot, 46
Barton, Dr., the Aeronaut, 49
Beads as Charms, 67
Bed of Otway Family, 55
Berlin, Archives of, 7
Bernhardt, Madame Sarah, 98
Bernora, Island of, 34
Beryl, 103, 119
Bettiscombe House, Skull at, 43
Beza, 103, 119
Bible at Spedlin's Tower, 66
Birth-month Stones, 128
"Black Sweep," Mascot, 100
Blavatsky, Madame H. P., 31, 160, 164
Blondlot, R., N-Rays of, 163
Bloodstone, 104, 120, 127, 136, 139
Bone of a Frog, 79
Boots, Charmed, 58
Bracelet of M. Santos Dumont, 14
Brazilian Pebble, 104
Breast-plate, Aaron's, 60
Brilliants, 104
British Museum, 53
Brooch, Tortoiseshell, 14
Buddhist Church, Strange Ceremony in, 73
Buddhist "Prayer Wheel," as a Mascot, 142
Bufonite, 104, 120
Bullet-proof Men, 56

Burmese Beliefs, 116
Burton Agnes Hall, Skull of, 41

Caaba, Stone of, 67
Cancer, Sign of, 127
Candles, Coughs Cured by, 81
Capricorn, Sign of, 128
Carbuncle, 104, 115, 120
Carnarvon, Lord, Charmed Tree of, 39
Carnelian, 31, 60, 85, 105, 114, 120, 134
Cast-off Clothing, 173
Cat, Civet, 79
Cats, Black, 49
Cattle of Chartley, 50
Cauls as Luck-bringers, 76
Caviglioli, Jean, 53
Chaka the Zulu King, 20
Chalcedony, 105, 126
Chalchihuitl, 105
Chameleon, 79
Charms—
    Artificial, 170
    Correct Method of Wearing, 145
    Dreams and, 88
    For Mental Development, 89
    For Protection from Animals, 90
    For Travellers, 89
    Historical, 4
    Jewels Classed as, 3

Charms—*Continued*
Magical, 173
National, 173
Natural, 173
Obsessed, 28, 178
Psalms as, 87
Writer's, 87
Written, 84–90
Chartley Cattle, 50
China, 17, 34, 93
— Empress of, 17
Chrysoberyl, 105
Chrysolite, 105, 120, 126, 128, 138, 139
Chrysoprase, 126
Clogs as Mascots, 100
"Coalstoun Pear," 39
Coat, Holy, of Treves, 63, 72
Coins, Charmed, 21, 22, 24, 142
Colouring of Gems, 182
Colours in Heraldry, 131
Colville, W. J., 164
Comb, Charmed, 78
Comtesse de Castiglione, 8
Coral, 105, 116, 120, 134
Coronation Stone, 32, 60, 93
Corsica, 53
Corundum, 105
Corvisart, Dr., 13
Countess D'Eu, 14
Cramp Rings, 80
Crocidolite, 106
Cromartie, Countess of, 54

Cromwell, Oliver, 54
"Crux Ansata," 68
Crystal, 106, 113, 116, 121, 131
Cuba, 21

Dalham Hall, 37
Darnborough, Mr. at Monte Carlo, 47
Days of Week and Gems, 130, 139
"Dead Hand" of Father Arrowsmith, 65
Dee, Dr., 35
Diamonds, 10, 19, 20, 28, 106, 114–6, 121, 131
Dog Trinkets, 100

Earrings, 60
Edenhall, Cup of, 26
Edward, Ring of King, 6
Egypt, 21, 67, 77
Egyptian Pebble, 107
Elector John of Brandenburgh, 6
Electrical Poles of Gems, 183
Elementals, 168, 176, 186
Ellenborough, Lady, and the Arabs, 30
Emerald, 10, 57, 107, 113, 115, 116, 121, 126, 127, 131, 137, 139
Ena, Princess, 25
England, 23, 26, 74

INDEX

Esty, Madame, 16
Evil Eye, 165
Experiments with Plants, 164

Family Charms, 92
Farjeon, B. L., the Novelist, 31
Feitsui, 107
Fire-stone, 107
Fitzgerald's, Sir Maurice, Black Cat, 49
Flags as Charms, 58, 94
Fox, 78
France, 4, 25, 40, 62
Frederick the Great, 7
French, Magic recognised by the, 4
Frog, 79, 134

Gabalis, Comte de, on Magic, 168
Garnet, 107, 122, 128, 136
Gem—
  Genesis of, 182
  Philosophers and, 180
  The Soul of a, 180
Gemini, The Sign, 127
German Emperor, 6, 49
Germany, 6
Gladstone, W. E., 50
Gnostics, 92, 178
Goblet as a Charm, 27
Gold Heart, 100
Gold Skull, 15

Grecian Beliefs, 113
Greece, 113
Grumbine, J. C. F., 164

Hadyn the Composer, 14
Haggard, Mr. Rider, 14
Hair, Human, 53, 77
Hall, Bryn, 65
— Burton Agnes, 41
— Dalham, 37
— Garswood, 66
— Hintlesham, 53
— Wardley, 44
Hand as a Charm, 65
Handkerchief, Curative, 60
Hare, 78
Hartmann, Dr., 164
Haunted Rooms, 41–5, 179
Hebrew Beliefs, 114
Heliotrope, 107
Heliotropian, 79
Henry VI., 27
Heraldry and Gems, 131
Herbs, 4, 79, 168, 174
Hindu Beliefs, 114
Hintlesham Hall, 53
Historical Charms, 4
Hohenzollern, House of, 6
Holy Coat of Treves, 63
— Hand, 65
— Land, 22
— of Holies, 18
— Vests, 61

Holy Water, 69, 72
Horseshoe, 56, 74–6, 100
House, Bettiscombe, 43
— Duchess of Alba's, 38
— Lord Revelstoke's, 37
— Lord Salisbury's, 37
— Unlucky, 36
Hufelans, Dr., 158
Human Beings as Mascots, 46-9, 82
— Blood, 183
— Rays, 164
— Will, 174, 187
Hyacinth, 107, 122, 126

Ikon, 66
India, 16, 19, 20, 51, 74, 114
Individual Charm, The, 91
"Isis Unveiled," 160
Italy, 165

Jacinth, 107
Jacob, 60
Jade, 17, 31, 99, 107, 122, 139
Janotha, Mdlle. Nathalie, 49
Japan, 77, 113
Japanese Beliefs, 113
Jargon, 107
Jasper, 108, 122, 126
Jerusalem, 6, 18, 126
Jewellery, 3-17, 80, 97-101, 130, 136, 141-4

Jews, 18, 76, 93, 114
Justin Martyr, 6

Kabala, 87, 92, 115, 133, 168
Kellermann, Miss, the Swimmer, 15
Keys, St. Peter's, 62
Kircher, Father, on Magic, 159, 163
Kite, 78
Knaresborough, Manor House, 44
"Koh-i-Noor" Diamond, 19
Koran, 28
Kruger, President, 20, 55
Kuropatkin's, General, Ikon, 66

Lamor, Miss Yvonne, 14
Lapis-lazuli, 108, 140
Leadbeater, Mr. C. W., 28, 164
Lee, The Penny of, 22
Leo, Sign of, 127
Libra, Sign of, 128
"Lincoln Imp," 142
Lockhart, Sir Simon, 22
Lodestone, 122, 183
Longworth, Mrs. Nicholas, 17
Luck, 4, 21, 47, 46, 53, 74, 184
Lucky Animals, 49
— Human Mascots, 46-9
— Names, 48, 84, 85

Madrid, Patron Saint of, 10]

Magic, 3, 4, 31, 114, 132, 134, 149-54, 158-60, 162, 174
Magic, Corner Stone of, 160
Magical Charms, 175
Magnetic Healing, 165
Magnetism, 177
Malachite, 108, 122
Manchurian Mascot, 35
Mandrake, 40
Man's Place in the Universe, 187
Mars, The Planet, 158, 186
Mascot, 3, 15, 16, 18, 27, 32, 35, 46, 47, 49, 51, 54, 93, 98-100, 141-3
Mecca, Blackstone of, 67, 92
Medal of St. Benoit, 14
"Mephisto's Ring," 10
Mesmer, 161
Metals, 4, 76, 132, 134, 135, 151, 158, 182, 185
Mexico, 113
"Mikko Monkey," 142
Monte Carlo, 47
Moonstone, 108, 114, 123
Morocco, 24
Moss-agate, 102
Mummy, 52, 99, 142, 179
Muncaster Mascot, 27
Musgrave, Sir Richard, 26
Mystery Animals, 78

N-Rays, 163

Names, 48
Napoleon I., 13
— III., 8
National Charm, 93
Natural Charms, 173
Nature Spirits, 166, 167
Necklace, Jade, 17
— of Vishnu, 115
"Nefer," 77
Nelson, 56
New Zealand, 31, 99
Nile Expedition, 13
North American Indians, 93
Numbers, 83, 178

Occult Jewellery, 101
"Od," 163
"Odylic Force," 163
Ojo de Buey, 108
Olcott, Colonel, 171
Olivine, 108, 123, 139
Onyx, 108, 133, 134, 140
Opal, 7, 15, 92, 109, 112, 113, 123, 128, 138, 139
Ophite, 109, 124
Original Motive for Wearing Jewellery, 3
Osiris, 68, 98
Otway Family, 55
Ox's Eye, 109

Pantacle, 134

Paracelsus on Talismans, 157, — 163

Parchment Charms, 61

Pear, Coalstoun, 39

Pearl, 109, 115, 124, 139

Pennington, Sir John, 27

Pentacle, 134

Peridot, 109, 124

Persia, 28

Pharaoh, 14

Philosophers and Magic, 152, 168, 180

Pipe, Charmed, 55

Pisces, The Sign, 128

Planetary Hierarchies, 187

Planets and their Gems, 128

Potato Charm, 82

Potet, Baron du, 176

Precious Stones, 4, 22, 60, 112, 115, 183

Psalms as Charms or Spells, 87-9

"Psychic Dynamo," 171

Rabbit as a Mascot, 51

Ramayana, Epic Poem of, 116

Reichenbach, 161, 164, 181

Religious Relics as Charms, 171

"Renown," Mascot of, 51

Revelstoke, Lord, 37

Ridgeway, Prof., on Jewellery, 3

Ring Apollonius of Tyana's, 5

Ring and Magic, 5

— Cramp, 80

— Cursed Spanish Opal, 7

— Czar of Russia's, 11, 12

— Fated, of Napoleon I., 13

— German Emperor's, 6, 92

— Hadyn's, 14

— in Westminster Abbey, 6

— King Edward's, 6

— Mephisto's, 10

— of Strength, 130

— Rider Haggard's, 14

— Solomon's, 5

— To prevent Falling Sickness, 6

Ripon, Marquis of, 54

Roman Beliefs, 113

Rosicrucians, 156

Rothschild, Leopold de, 31

— and Luck, 46

— Talisman, 57

Ruby, 10, 20, 109, 115, 116, 124, 127, 131, 137, 139

Russia, 11, 21, 22, 66, 67

Sagittarius, Sign of, 128

Salisbury, Lord, 37

Sapphire, 18, 93, 109, 114-6, 124, 126, 127, 131, 137, 139

Sardius, 126

Sardonyx, 110, 125, 126, 128, 134, 138

Scarab, 67

Schneider, Statement of, 7
Scorpio, Sign of, 128
Scorpion Charm, 86
Scotch Pebble, 110
Scott, Sir Walter, in "Talisman," 22
Seafield, Earl of, 39
Seal, Charmed, 15
— Planet's, 134
— Solomon's, 134
"Secret Doctrine," 160
Secret of Luck, 184
Selenite, 110, 139
Servia, 14
Seven, Number, 83
Seventh Son, 82
Siderite, 110
"Sistrum," 77
Skull, Burton Agnes Hall, 41
— Golden, 15, 91
— Knaresborough Manor, 44
— Screaming, 43
— Tunstead Farm, 43
— Wardley Hall, 44
Snake Stone, 110, 125
Snuff Box, 57
Socerer and Cardinal Wolsey, 6
Solomon's Ring, 5
— Seal, 30, 134
Spain, 8, 10, 24, 32, 81
Spanish American War, 7
— Opal, Cursed, 7

Spells, 4, 84–6
Spirits of Solomon, 5
St. Benoit, 14
St. Beuno, 70
St. Columbus, 33
St. Dunstan, 75
St. Edward, 32
St. John, 60
St. Peter, 62
St. Philomena, 72
St. Winefride, 69
Star Stone, 110
Stars and Stripes a Charm, 94
Stone, Coronation, 32, 60, 93
— Green Heart, 16
— of Bernora, 34
— of Caaba, 67
— of Iona, 34
— of Memphis, 110
— of Mukden, 34, 93
— Toad, of Germany, 7
— White, in Revelations, 61
Stonehenge, 33
Streeter, Mr., of Bond Street, 15

Table of Apostolic Virtues, 126
— of Birth-month Mascots, 143

Table of Gems, Metals, Names, and Designs, 135
— of Zodiacal Signs and Birth-stones, 127, 128
— to find Birth Gem, 129
Talisman, 22, 24, 39, 57, 132, 144, 157, 172, 175
Talmud, 87
Taurus, Sign of, 127
"Terrible Turk," Wears a Charm, 58
Tiger's Eye, 110, 125
Toad, 79
Toad-stone, 7, 92, 104
Tomb, Charmed, 62
Tooth, 79
Topaz, 16, 110, 125, 126, 128, 131, 134, 138
Topazolite, 111
Totems, 93
Tourmaline, 111
Trees, Charmed, 38
Treves, Holy Coat of, 63, 72
Tribal Charm, 92
Tunstead Farm, 43
Turquoise, 99, 105, 111, 125, 128, 138, 140
Tutnauer, Bernard, 22

Union Jack a Charm, 94
United States, 74
Universal Force, 161
Unlucky Cattle, 50

Unlucky Dalham, 37
— Houses, 36, 37
— Mummy, 52
— Names, 48
— Royal Sailors, 47
— Stream, 54
— Trees, 38, 39
Urim and Thummin, 60, 93

Vase, Charmed, 26
Vatican, Ring from the, 11
Verulam, Lord, 57
Vests, Holy, 61
Vibrations of Precious Stones, 174
Victoria, Queen, 20
Virgo, Sign of, 128

Wafers, Consecrated, 61
Wardley Hall, 44
Warts, Charming Away, 57
Watch-chain, Human Hair, 53
Water, 69, 72, 73
Wax Mask as a Charm, 53
Weapons, 28, 179
Weasel, 79
Wells, Holy, 69-72
Well, St. Winefride's, 69
— Lourdes, 72
— Mugnano, 72

INDEX

White Heather, 50, 100

William, Emperor, of Germany, 6, 49, 92

Williams, Hugh, a Lucky Name, 48

Winchelsea, Earl of, 38

Witchcraft, 165

Wolf, 79

Wolsey, Cardinel, Accused of Sorcery, 6

Yu-Chi, 111

Zodiac, 127, 135

Zulu Chief, 20

Zululand, 13